A SAMOAN READING OF DISCIPLESHIP IN MATTHEW

INTERNATIONAL VOICES IN BIBLICAL STUDIES

Editor
Monica Jyotsna Melanchthon
Jione Havea

Editorial Board
Musa W. Dube
David Joy
Andreas Kunz Lubcke
Aliou C. Niang
Nasili Vaka'uta

Number 8

SBL PRESS

A SAMOAN READING OF DISCIPLESHIP IN MATTHEW

by

Vaitusi Nofoaiga

 PRESS

Atlanta

Copyright © 2017 by Vaitusi Nofoaiga

Library of Congress Control Number: 2017958307

Printed on acid-free paper.

For my wife Mile, and our children:

Nofoaiga, Aliisolia, Victoria, Samuelu, Rosetta, and Eirenei;

and my loving parents:

Lealaiauloto Nofoaiga and Aliitasi Nofoaiga

CONTENTS

FOREWORD

Tautua is the Samoan word for serve, service, server and servant; *Tautua-i-le-va* refers to service that is rendered at a place which is in-between—this in-between place is the place of relations (*va*). *Tautuaileva* is the word that Nofoaiga coins for this service at the place of relations (or relational-places).

As an approach in biblical criticism, *tautuaileva* is complex. It is the fusion of several things:

1. It is about *service* (a) toward local people and local needs in which the *tautua* (server, disciple) (b) privileges "the crowd" (*tagata o le motu*) and villagers who tend to be marginalized, disadvantaged and ignored;
2. It is about *places* like (a) Galilee and (b) Samoa, which are overlooked by readers who are orientated toward Jerusalem and who prefer Western ways and values;
3. It is about *negotiating* values and relations (a) of local peoples at home and abroad and (b) of past and present Samoan societies;
4. It is about *intersecting*, in this study, (a) the roles of the Samoan *tautua*, (b) the Matthean notions of discipleship, (c) the Mediterranean first-century patriarchal world driven by systems of honor and shame and (d) Jesus's proclamation of ἡ βασιλεία τῶν οὐρανῶν (the kingdom of the heavens);
5. It is also about rethinking traditional understandings of (a) who counts among the disciples of Jesus and (b) what discipleship in Matthew involves.

With the twirlings and ebbings expected from an author who is a native of oral cultures, Nofoaiga holds the complexity of *tautuaileva* in this study and offers it as a contribution to the assembling/assembly of islander criticism. In that spirit, i draw attention to four critical moves that Nofoaiga makes in this study.

First, regarding *perspectives:* this study shows that the Bible (like other Scriptures) contains perspectives, and that there is no reason to privilege those over and against the perspectives of Samoan readers. It is not just readers who bring their perspectives to the act of reading; the Bible too brings its perspectives. The Bible is not innocent. It brings biases to the reading encounter.

Given that the Bible is a foreign book to Samoa, why should we expect Samoan readers to favour and uphold the biblical perspectives? The same question applies with respect to readers from (is)lands outside of the biblical land. Why do we priviledge biblical perspectives (read: hegemonies)? And when we are critical of readers and their perspectives, should we not also be critical of the Bible and its perspectives?

But then, why should the people of the biblical land uphold and privilege the biblical perspectives? This is the more critical question, seeing that the Bible has been used to justify the displacement of Palestinians and the occupation of their land.

Second, regarding *approaches:* this study shows that the perspective behind one approach in biblical criticism arose out of actual practices and life situations. Nofoaiga's approach is grounded (rather than imagined). *Tautuaileva* arises out of cultural and life struggles, and Nofoaiga draws upon the language (*gagana*), customs and traditions (*fa'asamoa*) of Samoa to situate his approach. In my humble opinion, this is a new form of nativism: Nofoaiga does not privilege or romanticize *fa'aSamoa* but uses it to sanction *tautuaileva* as a Samoan mode of reading.

Tautuaileva is not a "traditional" (old, ancient) Samoan practice but a "traditioning" (formative) Samoan mode of reading. In this way, Nofoaiga is not a cultural gatekeeper in the (old) nativist sense but a creative Samoan biblical critic in the cultural sense. It is for this reason that Nofoaiga could challenge, for example, the view held by the majority of Samoan Christians that discipleship is about putting God and the church before one's family. This study is thus critical of the Samoan mind and practices, through a Samoan study of different views of discipleship in Matthew.

Third, regarding the workings of *orality:* there is circularity in Nofoaiga's arguments, for two key reasons—he reads a text (e.g., Matt 4:12–15) through lenses (*fa'asinomaga* and *tautuatoa*) that look into and inform each other, and he uses the same lenses to read different texts (e.g., Matt 4:12–15 and Matt 7:24–8:22) within the same contexts (e.g., the narrative and rhetorical contexts of Matthew, the social and political contexts of the first century CE, and the traditional and current contexts of Samoa). Some repetitions are unavoidable, even with slight twists (that would still bore most readers who prefer linear arguments). But circularity and repetitions are characteristics of the oral preferring cultures behind both Matthew's text and Nofoaiga's Samoa.

Put another way, this study is another invitation to consider and engage the workings of orality: as the atmosphere *behind* the biblical texts, as the rhetorical device that holds the units *within* the biblical texts, as well as the verve that moves readers *in front* and *around* the biblical texts. Orality is not exhausted by textuality; orality can inspire dry texts. On orality, insofar as islander and biblical criticisms are concerned, more attention and work are needed.

Fourth, regarding the temptations to *contextualize and appropriate*: Nofoaiga does not deliver the usual contextual reading whereby something from his native culture is appropriated to make sense of, and thereby authorize (for both natives and foreigners), the biblical texts. Rather, his *tautuaileva* reading approach negotiates the (rhetorical) world encoded in the text of Matthew with the (sociohistorical) world of the first century CE in a way that it allows Nofoaiga, and other Samoan readers, to read in-between rigid historicism and formal literarism. There is hardly any benefit for Samoans to be involved in the historical or literary study of the Bible. The Bible is a foreign book to Samoa; and so are the principles and methods of historical and literary criticisms.

What worked for Nofoaiga is to start with Matthew as a rhetorical and narrative construction, and to use Samoan lenses (*fa'asinomanga* and *tautuatoa*) to seek out local people (in the text) and their responses to Jesus's proclamation of ἡ βασιλεία τῶν οὐρανῶν. Those who were affected by the proclamation and served (*tautua*) their various households are seen as disciples of Jesus. In this way, ἡ βασιλεία τῶν οὐρανῶν is not some imagined place removed from the lives and struggles of local people, whether in Galilee or in Samoa. Rather, in the in-between-space of *tautuaileva*, ἡ βασιλεία τῶν οὐρανῶν is already on earth. Not because of the proclamation of Jesus, but because of the responding service (*tautua*) of local people. And consequently, the disciples of Jesus were more than the usual twelve suspects.

Finally, this study is a healthy addition to the study of discipleship in Matthew, to biblical criticism in general and to islander criticism in particular.

Jione Havea
Wurundjeri country
13 April 2017

ACKNOWLEDGEMENTS

I am thankful to God for the guidance and protection while I undertook this study. While it is impossible to mention everyone who helped me in this task, I mention the following people whose patience and support enabled me to finish this study.

I express my great and sincere gratitude to Professor Elaine Mary Wainwright for her patience and wisdom, and to my friend Jione Havea for the encouragement and support.

Faafetai tele to my two mothers, Aliitasi Lealaiauloto Nofoaiga and Pualoa Faamausili Collins. Thank you for your prayers and fasting. Thanks also to all my brothers, sisters and families for your support.

Special thanks to the *tapuaiga* of my church, Congregational Christian Church Samoa, to Professor Otele Perelini and Reverend Maafala Lima, and to all my Malua colleagues, students and friends.

Last but not least, to my wife and children, thank you for your patience and care.

Faafetai, Faafetai Tele!

ABBREVIATIONS

AThR	*Anglican Theological Review*
BDAG	W. Bauer, W.F. Arndt, F.W. Gingrich, and F.W. Danker, *A Greek-EnglishLexicon of the New Testament and Other Early Christian Literature*
BibInt	*Biblical Interpretation*
BRev	*Bible Review*
BTB	*Biblical Theological Bulletin*
BZNW	Beihefte zur Zeitschrift für die neutestamentliche Wissenschaft und die Kunde der älteren Kirche
CBQ	*Catholic Biblical Quarterly*
CurTM	*Currents in Theology and Mission*
Di	*Dialog*
EBCE	*Encyclopaedia of Biblical & Christian Ethics*
EPT	*Encyclopaedia of Political Theory*
ERS	*Ethnic and Racial Studies*
FTh	*Feminist Theology*
HvTSt	*Hervormde teologiese studies*
Isa	Isaiah
JBL	*Journal of Biblical Literature*
JSNT	*Journal for the Study of the New Testament*
JSNTSup	Journal for the Study of the New Testament: Supplement Series
JFSR	*Journal of Feminist Studies in Religion*
LXX	Septuagint
Matt	Matthew
MSJ	*The Master's Seminary Journal*
MT	Masoretic text
NCBC	New Cambridge Bible Commentary
NICOT	New International Commentary on the Old Testament
NICNT	New International Commentary on the New Testament
NIGTC	New International Greek Testament Commentary
NIB	The New Interpreter's Bible
NovT	*Novum Testamentum*
NovTSup	Novum Testamentum Supplements
NRSV	New Revised Standard Version
NTL	New Testament Library
NT	New Testament
NTS	*New Testament Studies*

OED	*Oxford English Dictionary*
OT	Old Testament
OTL	Old Testament Library
PJT	*Pacific Journal of Theology*
RR	*Radical Religion*
SBL	Society of Biblical Literature
SCM	Student Christian Movement
Semeia	*Semeia*
SJTG	*Singapore Journal of Tropical Geography*
SNTSMS	Society for New Testament Studies Monograph
SPCK	Society for Promoting Christian Knowledge
TS	*Theological Studies*
WBC	World Biblical Commentary
WJK	Westminster John Knox
WUNT	Wissenschaftliche Untersuchungen zum Neuen Testament

GLOSSARY

Samoan words

aga	proper behaviour linked to social roles and appropriate contexts
aiga	family, relatives, extended family
ali'i	paramount or high chief
amataga	beginning
amio	actual behaviours of individuals as it emerges from personal drives and urges
fa'aaloalo	respect
fa'aiuga	ending
fa'amatai	chiefly system
fa'aSamoa	Samoan way
fa'asino	point or direct
fa'asinomaga	sense of belonging to a place
fale	house
feagaiga	a bond between two people or parties; the sister-brother relationship in *fa'aSamoa* is known as *feagaiga*
fealoa'i	interact respectfully
fuatia	hit or touch
ifo	bow
loto	person's will
maga	a suffix that makes a verb a noun, such as verb *fa'asino* as a noun, *fa'asinomaga*
matai	chief
ogatotonu	middle
palagi	European
sa'o	a chief chosen by the aiga as the family leader
si'osi'o	to round up
si'osi'omaga	environment
tau (verb)	relate, reach, fight, read, count
tau (noun)	weather, covering of traditional Samoan earth oven
tautai	fisherperson
tautua	serve, service, servant

tautuaileva	service in-between spaces
tautuatoa	courageous service/servant
toa	courageous
tulafale	orator or talking chief
tua	back or back space
tuaoi	boundary
tufuga	builder
umu	cooking food in a traditional earth oven
va	space (between parties, people, objects)
va-o-mamanu	inner-textures

Samoan phrases

amio fa'aaloalo	respectable behaviour
fatuaiga tausi	role of a family member
loto fuatiaifo	subjectivity, initiative
loto maulalo	humble, humility
malosi o le aiga ma le nu'u	the strength of the family and village
mamanu fa'a-agafesootai	social and cultural textures
o le tagata ma lona fa'asinomaga	the person and his/her sense of identity
siomiaga fa'atusiga	rhetorical and/or narrative unit
tamaiti sa	sacred children; in the sister-brother relationship the brother looks upon her sister's children as sacred because she is *feagaiga*
tautua fa'asinomaga	social and cultural role of a *tautua* as his or her sense of belonging to a place or family
tautua i le va	undertaking service in-between spaces or a servant standing in-between spaces
tautua le pa'o or *tautua le pisa*	to serve with silence
tautua tausi va e iloa le va fealoa'i	a service that respects the space between members of the family
tua atu o i	beyond this point
tulaga maota or *laoa*	residential place of a chief in the village
va fealoa'i	relationship
va-o-mamanu mai fafo	inter-textures

INTRODUCTION

This study offers interpretations of Jesus's ministry, as presented in Matthew, as exemplifying discipleship in a particular place, the Galilee. Since service is located, discipleship is not simply about service(s) to patron(s); discipleship also involves engaging at specific placements. It thus makes sense that an analysis of discipleship takes into account the placement of the service(s) rendered, realizing that service also takes place at in-between-places, and that the reader is shaped by services experienced at his/her personal placement.

This study analyzes the Matthean perspectives on discipleship employing a *tautuaileva*[1] (service in-between spaces) hermeneutics[2] that witnesses to my belonging, through my service (*tautua*), in Samoan societies. I belong to a place (Samoa) through my service (*tautua*). In this regard, placement has to do with the performance of duties (roles). The *tautuaileva* hermeneutics presented in this work is my contribution toward the development of islander criticism.[3] My contribution is of course located, hence limited, and I do not expect that it will be relevant to all islander readers.

In the reading that I offer in this work, I seek the conversion of the Matthean perspective of discipleship to make sense of Jesus's proclamation of ἡ βασιλεία τῶν οὐρανῶν (the kingdom of the heavens) in my world—contemporary Samoan societies at home and in diaspora. I use "conversion" not in the sense of imposing my Samoan world on the Matthean text, but creating a "convers-ation" between my experience of serving local Samoan people in local Samoan societies with the notion of discipleship embedded in a local world as encoded in the Matthean texts.

Why This Study?

Several reasons invite this study. First, this study is prompted by my experience that some social, cultural, and economic problems among Samoan families (at

---

[1] *Tautuaileva* combines the Samoan phrase *tautua i le va* into one word, to label my hybrid (in-between) location as a reader. I explain this further in chapters one and three.

[2] This phrase is jarred in English but that is the very nature of "third space" emphasised in this study to identify my location as reader. It shifts me as a reader to a new space. I explain this shift in details in chapter three.

[3] See Jione Havea, Margaret Aymer, and Steed Vernyl Davidson, eds., *Islands, Islanders, and the Bible: RumInations* (Atlanta: SBL Press, 2015) and Jione Havea, ed., *Sea of Readings: The Bible in the South Pacific* (Atlanta: SBL Press, forthcoming).

home and abroad) are due to our people's utter commitment to church duties as more important than caring for family needs. I have witnessed and heard of families struggling and blaming the gospel as a result. Jesus's teaching on the prioritizing of responsibilities and duties to church (read: discipleship) thus needs attention, in order to bring forth insights that can enable critical discussion of this subject in Samoan societies, as well as in other societies that struggle with the effects of this church-first ideology.

Second, the contentions in biblical studies concerning Jesus's attitude towards the family in relation to discipleship begs for a study like this one. This is because attention has tended to focus on Jesus's ministry in terms of its global function,[4] and less on Jesus's connection to family and household at a local level. As Halvor Moxnes suggests,

> His [Jesus] origin in terms of place and household has not evoked much interest. The question of his family is mostly relegated to a less important biographical interest. In a similar manner his critical elements about family and household, and about leaving family, become just a topic, and not a very important one, in the overall picture of Jesus' message. This seems to be typical of recent Christian scholarship on Jesus.[5]

Most of the studies on Jesus's attitude towards family in relation to discipleship use traditional methods of interpretation. This study offers an interpretation that focuses on the interaction between the world encoded in the text and my world as a reader of the Bible in contemporary Samoan societies (esp. in Samoa and in Aotearoa New Zealand).

Third, the contextual study of the Bible and its interpretations clears a place for me to undertake this work.[6] Despite the contextual and cultural peculiarities

---

[4] Examples are Stephen C. Barton, *Discipleship and Family Ties in Mark and Matthew*, SNTSMS 80 (Cambridge: Cambridge University Press, 1994); Martin Hengel, *The Charismatic Leader and His Followers*, trans. James C. G. Greig (Edinburgh: T&T Clark, 1981), 14–15; Gerd Theissen, *The First Followers of Jesus: A Sociological Analysis of the Earliest Christianity*, trans. John Bowden (London: SCM, 1978), 10–14; Ulrich Luz, *Matthew 1–7*, trans. James E. Crouch (Minneapolis: Fortress, 2007), 200–201. See also chapter 1.

[5] Halvor Moxnes, *Putting Jesus in His Place: A Radical Vision of Household and Kingdom* (Louisville: Westminster John Knox, 2003), 23.

[6] Contextual interpretation of the Bible is one of the more recent approaches to reading the Bible, mainly among readers whose worlds—such as African, Asian, and Islanders readers—are considered unimportant. Different terms were coined to define their reading, e.g., the African scholar Justin Ukpong uses "inculturation hermeneutics" (Justin Ukpong, "Inculturation Hermeneutics: An African Approach to Biblical Interpretation," in *The Bible in a World Context*, ed. Walter Dietrich and Ulrich Luz [Grand Rapids: Eerdmans, 2002], 17–32) and R.S. Sugirtharajah's uses "vernacular hermeneutics" (See

of my Samoan world, this work contributes not only to studies undertaken by other scholars on Jesus and family in Matthew, but also to the development of theories and methods of biblical interpretation in Samoa,[7] in particular, and in the shadows of islander criticism, more broadly.

Fourth, having witnessed first-hand the struggles of theology students in Samoa and in neighboring Pacific islands with how to layout a reading methodology that is relevant to their worlds, this study provides an example of a reading methodology that could be used, alongside methodologies proposed by other Samoan biblical scholars,[8] which utilizes Samoan culture and language.

R. S. Sugirtharajah, "Vernacular Resurrections: An Introduction," in *Vernacular Hermeneutics*,ed. R. S. Sugirtharajah [Sheffield: Sheffield Academic, 1999], 11–17).

Because the contextual dimension in my reading considers my own existence in today's world, I prefer the term "contextual" for the type of reading I am doing. I follow Nasili Vaka'uta's lead: "contextualizing interpretation and contextualizing the Bible are two separate tasks. The former is about employing contextual or, more specifically, indigenous categories of analysis for interpretation, whereas the latter is about applying the insights from one's reading to one's situation or tracing correspondence between a text and one's context. One is about methodology; the other is application" (Nasili Vaka'uta, *Reading Ezra 9–10 Tu'a-Wise: Rethinking Biblical Interpretation in Oceania* [Atlanta: Society of Biblical Literature, 2011], 2) My study does both. I employ Samoan indigenous references and apply them to a reading of the text. I would like to acknowledge here the leading biblical scholar in this type of reading in Oceania, a Tongan, Jione Havea. Examples of his works include "The Future Stands Between Here and There: Towards an Island(ic) Hermeneutics," *PJT* 2 (1995): 61–68; "Shifting the Boundaries: House of God and Politics of Reading," *PJT* 2 (1996): 55–71; and "Numbers," in *Global Bible Commentary*, ed. Daniel Patte (Nashville: Abingdon, 2004), 43–51.

[7] In chapter three I review some of the contextual biblical studies by Samoan scholars in order to situate my own Samoan perspective. I will not review studies by other Pacific or Oceanic biblical scholars out of respect for their own cultures. Talking about how other Oceanic scholars use their cultures or situations in their studies will not clarify how I use my culture and situation in my study. For example, Vaka'uta's work mentioned above is based on his perspective as a "Tu'a" in Tongan culture. According to Vaka'uta, Tu'a is a social and cultural class which he refers to as commoner. Once one becomes a Tu'a he or she will always be a Tu'a. In our Samoan culture we do not have a social and cultural class system. We have a *faamatai* (chiefly system) which is also a hierarchal system. In that system, its lowest rank is *tautua* which I use in my study to identify who I am as Samoan. *Tautua* as the lowest rank in the Samoan chiefly system is not a social and cultural class. It is the beginning stage upon which a Samoan makes his or her way up the ladder of the chiefly system to become a chief to lead the family and village one day. This example of different cultures in Oceania underpins my deciding to dialogue only with Samoan biblical scholars.

[8] I follow the lead by Peni Leota and Frank Smith in developing methods of interpretation that are contextual and relevant to the reading of the Bible from a Samoan perspective. See Peni Leota, "Ethnic Tensions in Persian-Period Yehud: A Samoan Postcolonial Her-

This work offers an approach that is rooted in the Samoan context, and it has implications for readers from other contexts, near and far.

Why Matthew's Perspective?

My focus on this study is Matthew's perspective on discipleship. Michael J. Wilkins suggests that Matthew's presentation of Jesus's ministry shows more clearly than any other gospel the nature of discipleship and this is manifestly told in the beginning and ending of Matthew's account.[9] It begins with the calling of the first disciples to leave their families to follow Jesus (Matt 4:18–23), and concludes with the great commissioning of the followers to go and make disciples of all nations (Matt 28:16–20). The frames of the book establish that discipleship is a major concern in the Matthean perspective. Through the course of the Matthew's account, the list of disciples grows from a selected few to a crowd.

I am making a controversial move in referring to this so-called gospel as an account with many perspectives. Many generations of contextual critics have seen the biblical text as "gospel" but the wisdom and traditions of our people (in Samoa, but also throughout the so-called third world) as "perspective." My hope in this move is to invite conversation on the fact that the gospels also contain perspectives and that the Samoan perspectives are good news also.

The underlying questions behind this work include: Which perspectives needs to be converted? Do Samoan perspectives need to be converted into or under the biblical perspectives or do the biblical teachings need to be converted under the Samoan perspectives? How might we move forward with contextual interpretation in Samoa, as well as in other (is)lands of Oceania and beyond?

Why Discipleship?

According to Fernando F. Segovia, the many interpretations and claims of what discipleship means to Matthew ultimately lead to two general definitions. First,

---

meneutic," (PhD Thesis, Melbourne College of Divinity, 2005) and Frank Smith, "The Johannine Jesus from a Samoan perspective: Towards an Intercultural Reading of the Fourth Gospel" (PhD Thesis, University of Auckland, 2010).

[9] Michael J. Wilkins, *The Concept of Disciple in Matthew's Gospel: As Reflected in the Use of the Term μαθητής* (Leiden: Brill, 1988), 2. Richard A. Edwards agrees that "almost all scholars assume that the author or redactor has a unified view of the disciples which is expressed consistently and evenly throughout the book" (Richard A. Edwards, "Uncertain Faith: Matthew's Portrait of the Disciples," in *Discipleship in the New Testament*, ed. Fernando F. Segovia [Philadelphia: Fortress, 1985], 47). Matthew was popular for church fathers such as Tertullian, Irenaeus, Clement of Alexandria, Origen and Augustine (see David F. Farnell, "The Synoptic Gospels in the Ancient Church: The Testimony to the Priority of Matthew's Gospel," *MSJ* 10 [1999]: 53–86).

discipleship (in the narrow sense) is a tradition of following Jesus in accordance with the historical master-disciple relationship between Jesus and his followers. Second, discipleship (in the broader sense) is the self-understanding of a Christian believer in relation to his or her daily practising of the teachings of Jesus.[10] Segovia's second definition points to the importance of considering the location of the reader in today's world. Someone who lives life today in the ways advocated by Jesus are also disciples.

Segovia's definitions allow for taking *Matthew's interpretation* of the master-disciple relationship to consolidate the audience's faith and to make sense within their daily lives. This "Matthew's interpretation" is what I call the "Matthean Perspective" in this work. In this way, one of the goals of the present study is to develop greater understanding of and appreciation for a reader's self-understanding and experience as a believer. My self-understanding of discipleship is based on my enculturation in the *fa'aSamoa* (Samoan way)[11] of *tautua* (serve, service, servant) that is learned and practiced in Samoan families and village communities. This understanding is expanded by my learning of the inclusive nature of Jesus's proclamation of ἡ βασιλεία τῶν οὐρανῶν ("the kingdom of heaven"). With this understanding I explore how Matthew's perspective presents discipleship as the task of following Jesus, in such a manner that I as a follower weave my understanding of Jesus's vision of ἡ βασιλεία τῶν οὐρανῶν to accord with the real world in which I live and struggle to survive.

---

[10] "In the latter sense, discipleship would be understood more generally in terms of Christian existence—that is, the self-understanding of the early Christian believers as believers..." (Fernando F. Segovia, "Introduction: Call and Discipleship—Toward a Re-examination of the Shape and Character of Christian Existence in the New Testament" in *Discipleship in the New Testament*, ed. Fernando F. Segovia [Philadelphia: Fortress, 1985], 2).

[11] *Fa'aSamoa* simply means "Samoan way." *Fa'aSamoa* can be regarded as Samoan cultural practices and rituals such as bestowal of title names, the Samoan social and cultural system, the chief/*matai* system, and the Samoan expected and accepted ways of behaving towards other people with respect (*fa'aaloalo*) regardless of who they are.

The *fa'aSamoa* show the connection between nature and culture in the Samoan world. This is evident in the words *āmio* and *aga*: "*Aga* refers to social norms, proper behaviour, linked to social roles and appropriate contexts. *Āmio* describes the actual behaviour of individuals as it emerges from personal drives and urges. [Thus] the ... term *āmio* focuses attention on the personal qualities of an act, whereas *aga* emphasises its social dimensions" (Bradd Shore in "Sexuality and Gender in Samoa: Conceptions and Missed Conceptions," in *Sexual Meaning: The Cultural Construction of Gender and Sexuality*, ed. Sherry B. Ortner and Harriet Whitehead [Cambridge: Cambridge University Press, 1981], 192–215). *Fa'aSamoa* is type of behaviour of a Samoan (*āmio*) which is in accordance with the Samoan social, cultural, and religious norms, roles, and statuses such as being a *tautua* or a *matai* (chief).

Studies that use traditional methods of interpretations to analyse the Matthean perspective on discipleship tend to focus on the global and ecclesiological functions of Jesus's ministry. The main characteristic of these interpretations is that disciples are men who are expected to abandon their families (parents, siblings, spouses and children) in order to become disciples to the world. Jerusalem, as the place where Jesus's ministry culminated in Jesus's death, burial, and resurrection, has been considered the most important place in defining the central message of discipleship. In that way, the importance of Galilee as the place where Jesus's ministry began is drawn into the historical and theological significance of Jerusalem.[12] The importance of Jesus's life and ministry in relation to those located in Galilee has received less attention. It is not that Galilee is unimportant, but that previous interpretations have not focussed on Galilee as a significant place in explaining the meaning of Jesus's ministry.

Considering Galilee as an important place in defining Jesus's ministry has recently received some attention,[13] mainly in the quest for the historical Jesus. One example is Halvor Moxnes's study which places Jesus in Galilee.[14] My study considers the importance of Galilee in regards to discipleship. Unlike Moxnes's study, I explore what Jesus's ministry means in terms of its relationship to the place of Galilee. My purpose is to see Jesus's ministry in place, in the Mediterranean Galilean world, as exhibited in the Matthean perspective. The goal is to uncover how the Matthean presentation of Jesus's relationship to vari-

---

[12] One example is reflected in Jack D. Kingsbury's threefold structure of Matthew's Gospel: (1) Matt 1:1–4:16 "Presenting Jesus to the reader," (2) 4:17–16:20 "Ministry of Jesus to Israel," (3) 16:21–28:20 "Jesus' journey to Jerusalem and of his suffering, death, and resurrection." See Jack D. Kingsbury, *Matthew as Story*, 2nd ed. (Philadelphia: Fortress, 1988), 129. The labelling of these three parts reflects the consideration of the ministry of Jesus as Son of God that culminated in Jesus's death, burial, and resurrection in Jerusalem as fulfillment of God's continuous love upon Israel. The function of Jesus as a Galilean does not play a major role in Kingsbury's interpretation.

[13] As Sean Freyne rightly said, "It is somewhat ironic, though inevitable that in an age of globalization recent studies of Jesus have been concerned with the local setting of his public life, thus giving rise to a renewed interest in Galilee also." Sean Freyne, *Jesus, A Jewish Galilean: A New Reading of the Jesus-Story* (London: T&T Clark International, 2004), 1. Freyne is one of the scholars leading the way in the study of the historical Jesus that focuses on the importance and significance of Galilee as a place in which Jesus's ministry took place.

[14] Moxnes, *Putting Jesus in His Place*. Other examples: Halvor Moxnes, "The Construction of Galilee as a Place for the Historical Jesus—Part I," *BTB* 31 (2001a): 26–37; Halvor Moxnes, "The Construction of Galilee as a Place for the Historical Jesus—Part II," *BTB* 31 (2001): 64–77; Sean Freyne, *Galilee, Jesus and the Gospels: Literary Approaches and Historical Investigations* (Philadelphia: Fortress, 1988). Sean Feyne, *Galilee and Gospel: Collected Essays*, WUNT 125 (Tübingen: Mohr, 2000).

ous and different members of the crowd, as local people, reveals other characteristics of discipleship that are pertinent to Galilee, as a local place.

Viewing Jesus's ministry in relation to its place in Galilee is prompted by
my identity and my place in the Samoan societies, where families live together
sharing social, cultural, and religious values and problems. My sense of identity
is social, cultural, religious and situational, shaped by my experience as a Samoan who has encountered both the margins and the centre of Samoan society. I
am aware of the problems in Samoan society, and their contradictions with certain values shared by our people. One example is the impact of the traditional[15]
characteristics of discipleship introduced into Samoa by missionaries.[16] One
traditional characteristic of discipleship is that a disciple should leave the family
and follow Jesus, with no expectation of a return. This implies that local family
needs and rights are secondary to the globally-emphasised one-directional focus
on building the global church. Discipleship, as such, contradicts the inclusive
nature of Jesus's proclamation of ἡ βασιλεία τῶν οὐρανῶν and egalitarianism in
social and cultural values as well as the practice of a *tautua* (serve, service, servant) in the Samoan social and cultural worlds. The arrival of Christianity into
Samoa in the 1830s brought colonial influences of the colonial powers at the
time such as Great Britain.[17] When the interpretation of leaving family to go and

---

[15] I distinguish between "traditional" in the teachings of missionaries versus "traditional"
according to *fa'aSamoa* which is significant to this study. "Traditional" in the missionaries' teachings stresses the global emphasis of discipleship. In *fa'aSamoa*, "traditional" is
reflected in the local emphasis of the Samoan culture defined by the word *aganuu. Aganuu* means ways and values pertaining to a particular context, such as a local village, a
nation or country.

[16] Traditional discipleship introduced by the missionaries into Samoa in the 1830s has
guided the practice of discipleship in Samoan society today. The Samoan people saw in
the Christian tradition a change that would improve their lifestyle. Despite many good
results of discipleship there were some failures, such as transforming the traditional and
cultural values of Samoans. See Malama Meleisea, *Lagaga: A Short History of Western
Samoa* (Suva: University of the South Pacific Press, 1987), 67–69. One of the changes
was the shift in the undertaking of *tautua* which affects how local people consider their
roles in relation to their family. For some Samoans in contemporary Samoan society, the
family-centered social, cultural, and religious roles of *tautua* are secondary to serving the
church. *Tautua* is a very important social and cultural status in the *Matai* (Chief) system.
See chapter two.

[17] Meleisea, *Lagaga*, 52–59; 67. Meleisea is a well-recognized Samoan historian. He
wrote the history of Samoa from a Samoan perspective. See also, R. P. Gilson, *Samoa
1830–1900: The Politics of a Multi-Cultural Community* (Melbourne: Oxford University
Press, 1970), 65–137. Gilson sees Samoan history from a European point of view. Oka
Fau'olo, *O Vavega o le Alofa Lavea'i: O le Tala Faasolopito o le Ekalesia Faapotopotoga Kerisiano i Samoa* (Apia: Malua Printing Press, 2005), wrote the history of
Christianity in Samoa from the perspective of a minister and theological teacher. While

make disciples of all nations was melded with colonialism, discipleship also became tied to colonialism. Traditional notion of discipleship is thus understood as a colonial practice. Discipleship, as such, is saturated with the patriarchal and hierarchical language of the Bible.[18] Patriarchy as a cultural system and androcentrism as a worldview nullified the *tautua* (service) orientation and shared-roles of men and women in Samoa; these are the roles that ensure peace and harmony in the community, according to which men and women should act in the interest of their families.[19]

This study engages Matt 4:12–25 and 7:24–8:22 using the *tautuaileva* (service in-between spaces) hermeneutics, investigating how Jesus's ministry in these texts attends to the needs and rights of local family members in Galilee. Because this study focuses on the world encoded in the text, I treat as significant the following three aspects of the local world of Galilee. First, I consider Jesus as a local of Galilee, and a servant who had the ability to bring out those in need from the colonial and oppressive systems of the local place of Galilee. Second, I treat Galilee as a local place in the first century Mediterranean world. And third, I analyse the diverse roles of the crowds for the ways they reflect situations in Galilee that Jesus addressed in his ministry. I consider anyone from the crowd whom Jesus helped in Galilee to have revealed discipleship as a place-based mission. In that way, this study will lay out another interpretation of discipleship that goes beyond the global one-directional and one-dimentional focus of traditional discipleship, with its inherent dualistic structure of becoming a disciple: the called/not called, chosen/not chosen, and male/female.

How This Study?

The study is divided into two parts. Part 1, *Tautuaileva* Hermeneutics, includes three chapters. Chapter 1 first gives a review of studies of discipleship that utilise traditional methods of interpretation. This demonstrates how they focus one-dimensionally on the global and ecclesiological aspect of discipleship; that is, they are concerned with spreading the word of God to the world as a mission to build the church at the global and ecclesiological level. This survey is followed

---

Meleisea speaks of the arrival of Christianity as a progressive mission, Fauolo sees it as the work of God.

[18] Wainwright shows how the Bible is patriarchal and androcentric in relation to Matthew. See Elaine M. Wainwright, *Towards a Feminist Critical Reading of the Gospel According to Matthew*, BZNW 60 (Berlin: de Gruyter, 1991), 27–28.

[19] I am aware of the marginalizing impact of the hierarchical Samoan chief system on the local people in Samoan local villages and communities. The scope of this study does not allow me to discuss this in details. My focus instead is on the negative impact of traditional discipleship on Samoan society and how it contradicts the egalitarian aspects of Samoan culture such as the culture of *tautua*.

by a discussion of a different group of readers whose interpretations of disciple-ship are explicitly shaped by their worlds as readers. The review of interpretations from this group reveals other characteristics of discipleship, such as the place of women among disciples. These reviews set the scene for my pro-posed *tautuaileva* reading which is shaped by my Samoan world and worldviews (identified and developed in chapters 2 and 3).

My proposed reading considers as important my location as a reader. Chap-ter 2 explains my location as third space. The entrance to this third space is determined by my identity as a member of a Samoan family, church and society, in which I am a *tautua* (servant). *Tautua* is a social and cultural status of a member of a Samoan family, as well as a family- and community-based social and cultural role and practice. Being *tautua* exhibits my role and responsibility to my family and church regardless of my gender, academic achievements and status as church minister and father. As such, *tautua* expresses my sense of place as a Samoan that determines how and why I enter (through service) the third space, which I call *tautuaileva*—service in-between. The exploration of my identity as Samoan begins by defining "identity" and "place" from a cultural and ethnic perspective, followed by my explanation of *tautua* as shaping that per-spective. Part of my role as *tautua* is to identify problems that hamper the fulfilment of that role and identify a pathway to address those problems. In sec-tion three of this chapter, I identify the problem that determines how I enter the third space. The overriding problems are marginalization and inequality, which in part, has been caused and exacerbated by the persistent teaching and practice of traditional discipleship in Samoan society. As a result, I enter the third space (considered in this study as a location in hybridity) as a place for service. The chapter concludes by specifying the categories of this location that will be uti-lised as hermeneutical lenses to read the Matthean texts.

Chapter 3 explains how my location in third space serves as a hermeneutical lens to inform the analyses of texts. I present my *tautuaileva* approach in the context of attempts by Samoan scholars to construct Samoan hermeneutics. My *tautuaileva* hermeneutics supplements those efforts. *Tautuaileva* has two k/ elements: *Faasinomaga* (belonging to a place) and *Tautuatoa* (courageous se ant), which are the categories that guide my reading of the selected texts.

Part 2: *Tautuaileva Readings* contains two chapters. In chapter 4 I ar Matt 4:12–25 as a rhetorical unit, exploring how Jesus's ministry to Gali encoded in the text) might be read through the lenses of *fa'asinomaga* (/ belonging to a place) and *tautuatoa* (courageous servant). This read/ primary attention to the needs and rights of local people, vis-a-vis the/ Section one discusses the inner texture of the text. Section two de/ Matthean recitation of Isa 8:23–9:1, which leads to a particular inte Jesus's ministry. Section three deals with the social and cultural te 4:12–25 which enables me to explore Jesus's proclamation of ?

οὐρανῶν in the context of the world of Galilee. I will examine whether Jesus's vision of ἡ βασιλεία τῶν οὐρανῶν makes meaning within the social and cultural worlds of the first century Mediterranean world with particular attention to the poor and marginalized. Can it be read as third space, a space where Jesus's vision of ἡ βασιλεία τῶν οὐρανῶν is proclaimed in accordance with the reality that local Galileans face? I will assess whether the proclamation of ἡ βασιλεία τῶν οὐρανῶν in the beginning of the Matthean text can be read as consideration of the needs and rights of local people.

The analysis of Matt 4:12–25 shows that Jesus's sense of belonging to Galilee is revealed in his making his home in Galilee, and in his proclaiming ἡ βασιλεία τῶν οὐρανῶν there. The continuation of that ministry is revealed in Jesus's dealing with other local Galileans in Matt 7:24–8:22, the text explored in chapter 5. In contrast to Matt 4:12–25, in Matt 7:24–8:22 Jesus takes his ministry to the houses and families of local people. The first section of this chapter will analyse the innertexture of Matt 7:24–8:22 as a rhetorical and narrative unit through *tautuaileva*, exploring how Jesus's ministry to the local families of Galilee reveals Jesus's attention to the needs and rights of local people. Section two offers an analysis of Matthew's recitation of Isa 53:4 in the literary context of Matt 7:24–8:22. This shows intertextually how attending to the needs of local people is a challenge that requires courage and endurance. In section three I analyse the social and cultural textures of the text exploring the first century Mediterranean social and cultural values of honor and shame, and Jesus's reversal of that value.

In the concluding chapter 6, I explain the three important features of this study. First, it presents an example of developing a method of biblical interpretation from an islander world—using the Samoan *tautuaileva*—to make sense of discipleship. Second, it proposes another interpretation of the Matthean perspectives on discipleship. Third, this study invites further attention to the role of the church in considering the needs and rights of local people.

This study thus suggests that Jesus's dealing with the needs and rights of local people is permission to deal with the reality of the world we are now encountering. It demonstrates the way local people as disciples or *tautua* of God and of their families should deal with their needs and rights as members of their families, churches, and communities. In this way, discipleship is to be carried out in accordance with the needs and rights of the people at the local level.

PART 1

TAUTUAILEVA APPROACH

1.

SITUATING *TAUTUAILEVA* READING

I first review some of the studies on discipleship that utilise traditional methods of interpretation. This review demonstrates that traditional readings focus on the global and ecclesiological aspect of discipleship, that is, they are concerned with discipleship as a means for spreading the word of God to the world as a mission to build the church at the global level.

This survey is followed by a discussion of interpretations of discipleship by biblical critics whose readings are shaped by their worlds. The differences in the interpretations between these two groups reveal other characteristics of discipleship, for example, consideration of the place of women among disciples. These two reviews set the scene for my proposed interpretive approach and resulting readings which are shaped by my Samoan context.

Traditional Approaches

Historical and literary criticisms are the dominant approaches in biblical criticism. The interpretations of discipleship[1] that they produce were and still are the mainline (read: accepted, authorized) meanings of discipleship. As Fernando F. Segovia observes,

> Since for historical criticism the text as means possessed a univocal and objective meaning and since this could be retrieved via a properly informed and conducted scientific inquiry, the meaning uncovered was for all times and cultures....In other words, the original meaning of the text, properly secured and established, could dictate and govern the overall boundaries or parameters of the Christian life everywhere and at all times.[2]

As examples of the use of traditional methods of interpretation, I survey the interpretations of the Matthean perspective on discipleship by four male European-American scholars: Martin Hengel, Gerd Theissen, Stephen Barton, and Ulrich Luz.

---

[1] These understandings of discipleship express the colonial ideologies of chosenness and exclusivism. See Musa W. Dube, *Postcolonial Feminist Interpretation of the Bible* (St. Louis: Chalice Press, 2000) 12–13, 17.

[2] Fernando F. Segovia, *Decolonizing Biblical Studies: A View from the Margins* (New York: Orbis, 2000), 14.

First, Martin Hengel uses historical criticism to study the historical Jesus and the nature of discipleship in the Christian religion. He brings the theme of "discipleship and family ties" in recent studies to the attention of biblical scholars as they relate to the gospels. Based on his interpretation of Matt 8:18–22, Hengel argues that Jesus's call for disciples to leave their families and follow him is not a call made in terms of a teacher-pupil relationship or of a prophetic role, but rather in terms of Jesus's messianic work as proclaimer of the impending kingdom of God.[3]

Hengel interprets Jesus's calling of the disciples (see Matt 8:21) in contrast to the scribe asking to follow Jesus in Matt 8:19–20.[4] For Hengel, the kind of discipleship Matthew emphasises is not a rabbinical type of discipleship (teacher-pupil relationship), which is portrayed by the scribe's request, but one that is eschatological, as exhibited in Jesus's answer to let the dead bury their own dead (Matt 8:22), which has to do with the spiritual being of the follower. Hengel's interpretation emphasises the eschatological significance of discipleship, and I take it as an example of the traditional notion of discipleship.

Hengel insists that Jesus expected the disciple whom he called to leave his family because the task of discipleship was not easy. Hengel compares this task to the hardship of Jesus's own messianic work. Hengel's interpretation, which is determined by Jesus's messianic character, emphasizes the importance of leaving home as a commitment to the global mission. To Hengel, this is one of the most significant historical events of discipleship in the Christian religion.

Second, Gerd Theissen uses a sociohistorical approach to demonstrate the historical nature of discipleship. He emphasizes the view of leaving home as commitment to undertake discipleship. Theissen sees the function of a disciple in Jesus's ministry as distinct, and this is shown in the comparison of two types of disciples.[5] One is the group called "itinerant charismatics" and the other is the group called "local less faithful."

The itinerant charismatics were a group of wandering disciples who, in following Jesus, abandoned all family ties as they moved around Palestine preaching the kingdom of God. As an example, Theissen points to the twelve disciples that Jesus sent on the mission to Israel in Matt 10:1–45.[6] According to Theissen, Jesus's answer to the scribe in Matt 8:20 anticipates the type of mission that will be undertaken by the twelve in Matt 10:1–45. It reveals the twelve as the wandering charismatics who will be homeless. Theissen interprets the

---

[3] Hengel, *The Charismatic Leader*, 15.

[4] Ibid., 14–15.

[5] Gerd Theissen, "Itinerant Radicalism: The Tradition of Jesus' Sayings from the Perspective of the Sociology of Literature," *RR* 2 (1975): 84–93.

[6] Gerd Theissen, *The First Followers of Jesus: A Sociological Analysis of the Earliest Christianity*, trans. John Bowden (London: SCM, 1978), 10–14.

sending out of the twelve in Matt 10:1–45 to undertake a wandering life in discipleship as showing the loss of family and lack of possessions expected of the disciples of Jesus. Theissen considers this group the authentic followers of Jesus.

The local less faithful is the inactive group which is made up of those who did not want to make the commitment to leave home. Theissen's use of structural functionalism signifies the function of the called disciples as family members but does not explicitly mention the kinds of situations to which he was referring.

Third, Stephen Barton undertakes a historical survey of the subordination of family ties in Judaism and in the Greco-Roman world of the first century. He focuses on discipleship and family ties in Mark and Matthew in his survey. He claims that sufficient evidence exists from the first century Mediterranean world to suggest the importance of leaving families in pursuit of a higher and advanced role or of a household standing.[7] Barton interprets the "call" stories in Matt 4:18–22 and Mark 1:16–20 as the disciples' commitment to Jesus over their own social and cultural world: "the in-breaking of the kingdom of heaven and the call to follow Jesus establish priorities which transcend the mundane obligations of occupation and family life."[8] Barton espouses the subordination of family ties in Matthew as key to becoming a disciple. He adds that Matthew's revelation of Jesus's calling of family members to leave their families is christologically and eschatologically based. Barton's conclusion shows that the subordination of family ties in Christian belief is necessary in order to reach the higher household of God.

One of the problems with the traditional methods is how to determine the correct interpretation. This is evident in the work of the fourth scholar in this survey, Ulrich Luz's study of disciples in Matthew. Using literary criticism, Luz begins his study by setting out two kinds of interpretations of disciples in Matthew.[9] One is characterized by "transparency" and the other by "historicizing."[10] According to Luz, these different interpretations of discipleship are problematic.

---

[7] Stephen C. Barton, *Discipleship and Family Ties in Mark and Matthew*, SNTSMS 80 (Cambridge: Cambridge University Press, 1994), 23–56.

[8] Ibid., 139.

[9] Other literary studies of discipleship in Matthew are Kingsbury, *Matthew as Story*; Richard A. Edwards, *Matthew's Narrative Portrait of Disciples: How the Text-Connoted Reader Is Informed* (Harrisburg: Trinity Press International, 1997); Daniel Patte, *Discipleship according to the Sermon on the Mount* (Valley Forge: Trinity Press International, 1996); Warren Carter, "Matthew 4:18–22 and the Matthean Discipleship: An Audience-Oriented Perspective," *CBQ* 59.1 (1997): 58–75; David B. Howell, *Matthew's Inclusive Story: A Study in the Narrative Rhetoric of the First Gospel*, JSNTSup 42 (Sheffield: Sheffield Academic, 1990), 53.

[10] Ulrich Luz, *Studies in Matthew*, trans. Rosemary Selle (Grand Rapids: Eerdmans, 2005), 115–17.

He challenges studies on discipleship that accentuate the historicizing aspects and argues that the problem with historicizing characterization is that it speaks of "disciples" as a historical character group whose function remains in the past.[11]

Luz prefers the "transparency" characterization which allows him to refer to "disciples" as an ecclesiological term. He claims that the "ecclesiological dimension evidently belongs to the history of the proclamation and of the ministry of Jesus."[12] This claim is reflected in Luz's interpretation of Matt 4:12–22 where he considers Galilee as the "place of the origin of the [church] community."[13] In this way, Luz's emphasis on discipleship as the building of the church asserts that all followers of Jesus are commissioned to the global mission.[14] Like the other interpretations surveyed above, Luz's interpretation is based on the one-directional global focus of discipleship.

In this survey of the studies by Hengel, Theissen, Barton, and Luz as examples of interpretations that use traditional methods,[15] I find that they conform to the view that discipleship is a mission in which followers of Jesus must leave

---

[11] Luz wrote that Strecker's historicizing interpretation of disciples in Matthew suggests that Matthew identifies the disciples with "the twelve." He said that Strecker's interpretation is based on Matthew's filling out of Mark's frequent use of δώδεκα (twelve) with μαθηταὶ (disciples). Luz argues that "this (Strecker's interpretation) warns us to be careful: if Matthew can omit Mark's δώδεκα and replace it with μαθηταὶ, this shows not that the number of the disciples was important to him but that he took the number for granted. Above all, Matthew never replaces μαθηταὶ in his tradition with δώδεκα μαθηταὶ (twelve disciples)." Hence, Luz concludes that Strecker's interpretation does not elucidate the meaning of disciples in Matthew (Luz, *Studies in Matthew*, 116–17).

[12] Luz, *Matthew 1–7*, 200–201.

[13] Ibid., 14.

[14] Luz claims that "what Matthew receives from Mark's Gospel is a *report* of the commissioning. In Mark the disciples actually are sent out and later return (6:30). Luke constructs the commissioning similarly as a report on the seventy disciples.... Matthew expressively did not construct the commission as a report of a singular event in the past. We could overstate this by saying that Jesus instructs his disciples but does not actually send them out" (Luz, *Studies in Matthew*, 146, 150–51). According to my underscoring of the Matthean story of Jesus's ministry, the commissioning of the twelve is Jesus's sending them back to their families after they have learned from the Sermon on the Mount and Jesus's healings that will help them improve their houses/households. Their meeting with Jesus in the beginning of chapter twelve, where they are described by the narrator as hungry disciples, shows that their return to their families in chapter ten was not an easy task.

[15] Other examples of studies of the nature of disciples which used the historical approach: Sjef Van Tilborg, *The Jewish Leaders in Matthew* (Leiden: Brill, 1972); and Paul S. Minear, "The Disciples and the Crowds in the Gospel of Matthew," *AThR* 3 (1974): 28–44.

their families to go and make disciples of all nations. Determined by the use of traditional methods, these interpretations serve the global purpose of discipleship well.

However, some aspects of those traditional interpretations do not reflect the reality of life encountered by Christians in the twenty-first century. One example is the aspect of leaving the family and following Jesus as if there is no return. This aspect overlooks the importance of local situations encountered by local families left behind. I address this in my *tautuaileva* reading below.

The use of traditional methods in interpreting discipleship in Matthew will continue to bear the global focus of discipleship. Those interpretations will continue to overlook the inclusive nature of Jesus's vision of ἡ βασιλεία τῶν οὐρανῶν as defined within the various situations encountered by local people in local contexts. And this continues to have a great impact on how Christians practice discipleship in their life situations. On this issue, Sugirtharajah writes,

> biblical studies is still seduced by the modernistic notion of using the rational as a key to open up texts and fails to accept intuition, sentiment, and emotion as a way into the text. By and large, the world of biblical interpretation is detached from the problems of the contemporary world and has become ineffectual because it has failed to challenge the status quo or work for any sort of social change.[16]

Traditional interpretations of discipleship as products of historical, sociohistorical, and literary criticisms are important because they reveal the global function of discipleship. However, they overlook how that global function is defined within the local, the social, cultural, economic, political, and religious situations of people in the world encoded in the text, and in the world of real readers. An analysis of these concerns have been made possible by new methods of interpretation, such as the approaches that are shaped by the world of readers and their hermeneutical perspectives.

Approaches that Affirm the Location of Readers

Considering the reader's situation as important, Fernando F. Segovia speaks of the location of meaning as an encounter between text and reader.[17] This differs from the traditional approaches which locate meaning in the worlds of the author

---

[16] R. S. Sugirtharajah, *Postcolonial Criticism and Biblical Interpretation* (Oxford: Oxford University Press, 2002), 26.

[17] Fernando F. Segovia, "Cultural Studies and Contemporary Biblical Criticism: Ideological Criticism as Mode of Discourse," in *Reading From This Place: Social Location and Biblical Interpretation in Global Perspective*, ed. Fernando F. Segovia and Mary Ann Tolbert, vol. 2 (Minneapolis: Fortress, 1995), 1–17.

and of the (original) text. This shift has raised questions regarding how the prac-
titioners and proponents of the traditional methods of biblical criticism, who
came from a wide range of social and geographical locations, overlooked the
perspectives and agendas of readers. Readings are necessarily affected by readers's social, cultural, economic, religious and political locations and situations.

A number of studies affirming personal location emerged in the mid-1970s
in which approaches in "cultural criticism" (Segovia) and "vernacular hermeneutics" (Sugirtharajah) were developed and institutionalized into the
mainstream of biblical studies.[18] This shift in biblical interpretation brought
changes to the interpretations of discipleship. These studies were the beginning
of explorations into discipleship which pay attention to local situations and local
people.

Feminist criticism, as the most prominent among those approaches, is a
well-known form of biblical criticism which engages the text and challenges
dominant methods of interpretation through the filters of social and political
concerns, and the interests of women.[19] Feminist readers insist on reading discipleship through a lens that opens up the potential for reading women as disciples
of Jesus.[20] For example, Elaine M. Wainwright's study, using the literary-
historical method, constitutes a critical reading of Matthew from a feminist perspective which recognizes the voices of marginalized women in the text. Her
inclusive interpretation of the crowd's following in Matt 4:25 and its link to the
healing of Peter's mother-in-law (Matt 8:14–15) and the woman with haemorrhages (Matt 9:20–22), shows a significant difference from the exclusive
interpretations of discipleship made by the male European-American scholars
surveyed above.

The male studies of discipleship restrict the calling of Jesus's disciples to
the twelve, which includes the four fishermen in Matt 4:18–22. Wainwright on
the other hand argues that the crowd in Matt 4:25 are similar to the four fisher-

---

[18] See Fernando F. Segovia, "And They Began to Speak in Other Tongues: Competing
Modes of Discourse in Contemporary Biblical Criticism," in *Reading from This Place:
Social Location and Biblical Interpretation in the United States*, ed. Fernando Segovia
and Mary Ann Tolbert, vol. 1 (Minneapolis: Fortress, 1995), 1–34. See also R. S.
Sugirtharajah, ed., *Vernacular Hermeneutics* (Sheffield: Sheffield Academic Press,
1999).

[19] For an overview of feminist criticism's directions and influence in Matthean studies,
see Elaine M. Wainwright, "Feminist Criticism and the Gospel of Matthew," in *Methods
for Matthew*, ed. Mark Allan Powell (Cambridge: Cambridge University Press, 2009),
83–117.

[20] See also Janice Capel Anderson, "Matthew: Gender and Reading," *Semeia* 28 (1983):
3–27, and Elizabeth Schüssler Fiorenza, *Discipleship of Equals: A Critical Feminist
Ekklesia-ology of Liberation* (London: SCM, 1993).

men in Matt 4:20, except that the crowd does not indicate gender differences.[21] The crowd must have included both women and men who responded positively to Jesus's ministry. Other women disciples include Peter's mother-in-law (Matt 8:14–15) and the woman with haemorrhages (Matt 9:20–22). According to Wainwright, the healing of Peter's mother-in-law (Matt 8:14–15) points out a member of the crowd whose mission is to serve Jesus in her household and beyond.[22] Peter's mother-in-law is another disciple of Jesus.[23]

Postcolonial critics also consider discipleship in relation to the readers' world. The Botswanan scholar Musa W. Dube also insists on reading for social liberation as a woman but with a postcolonial emphasis. She finds evidence of colonialism in the spread of Christianity. Christianity has been exclusivist, and contradictory to the goals of Jesus's ministry. This problem is shown in and through the connection between missionaries, Bible readers, and their Christian institutions. It allows readers in the postcolonial era to take a new approach that is meaningful and appropriate to them. For Dube, such a connection enables readers to illuminate the meaning and implications of the text within a postcolonial context.

In Dube's reading of Matt 28:19a, she analyses the command *to make disciples of all nations* as part of an ideology that bolsters and encourages imperialism.[24] She relates this interpretation to her own situation as a well-travelled African woman scholar.[25] Based on that experience, Dube claims that "the command (*to make disciples of all nations*) not only instructs Christian readers to travel to all nations but also contains a 'pedagogical imperative'...."[26] The commissioning of disciples gives the traveller authority not only to trespass on other nations but also to proclaim the Christian message as more important than the nation's beliefs. This command on the one hand requires other nations to listen to the disciples' message, and on the other hand suggests that other worldviews are not worthwhile. Dube found that in her case as a student, who travelled to Great Britain (for her masters) and the United States (for her PhD) for theological and biblical studies, the expectation was that she would be "dis-

---

[21] Wainwright, *Towards a Feminist Critical Reading*, 80–81.

[22] Ibid., 83–87.

[23] In other words, this woman's serving Jesus makes her a disciple on behalf of Jesus. Wainwright suggests that her service is indication of "going beyond."

[24] Dube, *Postcolonial Feminist Interpretation*, 157–95.

[25] Ibid., 130–35. Dube interprets other events in Matthew, such as "tax issues and the trial of Jesus," as illustrating that the Matthean is imperialist.

[26] Musa W. Dube, "'Go Therefore and Make Disciples of All Nations' (Matt 8:19a): A Postcolonial Perspective on Biblical Criticism and Pedagogy," in *Teaching the Bible: The Discourses and Politics of Biblical Pedagogy*, ed. Fernando F. Segovia and Mary Ann Tobert (Maryknoll: Orbis, 1998), 224.

cipled by them."[27] Thus, she considers the imperial sense of the command "to make disciples of all nations" as conforming to the imperial expansion of American and European powers.

Dube regards the Bible as an imperialist text. She observes that, "the future course and role of biblical criticism must be informed by our own *history*, our own experience, and our quest for cultural and economic liberation."[28] Dube, unlike other interpreters of discipleship, places colonialism at the centre of the biblical text and considers the Matthean text as an imperialist text. The discussion of imperialism and colonialism by Dube is in relation to European imperial and colonial expansion into Africa, which she claims was helped by the imperial language of the biblical text.

The readings by Wainwright and Dube signify who they are as readers. Wainwright interprets the text from her perspective as a woman disciple of Jesus. Dube looks at the text from her position as an African woman in the previously colonized world of Africa. She considers the Bible to be an imperial text whose language and interpretations contributed to the colonization of Africa. Wainwright and Dube attempt to make sense of Jesus's ministry in relation to who they are in their own contexts. This aspect is crucial in my proposed reading proposed below.

Sociorhetorical Approaches

In light of Gadamer's aesthetic theory (see chapter three), according to which the text has a world of its own, I take the world(s) encoded in the Matthean account of Jesus's ministry as local world(s). I will thus explore how the language of the text tells and shows particular events that reveal the links of Jesus's ministry to the local world. That world is revealed narratively by the people, their relationships with each other, and how the systems that run and control that world influence those relationships. Because sociorhetorical criticism as a reading method focuses on the world encoded in the text, I have chosen it as the interpretational tool with which to construct my *tautuaileva* hermeneutic.

Vernon K. Robbins developed sociorhetorical criticism as the integration of a social science approach with literary-based advances in biblical studies.[29] His goal was to develop a rhetorical approach that combined literary, social, cultural, and ideological issues in the interpretation of biblical texts. Sociorhetorical criti-

---

[27] Ibid., 226.
[28] Ibid., 228.
[29] Vernon K. Robbins, *Exploring the Texture of Texts: A Guide to the Socio-rhetorical Interpretation* (Harrisburg: Trinity Press International, 1996), 1.

cism recognizes that a world is encoded in the text in and through its language.[30] Sociorhetorical criticism provides tools for interpreters to examine how the text's language shape meanings, and allows readers to relate those meanings with their own world in order to make meaning relevant.[31] Readers with different insights from diverse locations may interpret the same text.[32] In this way, sociorhetorical criticism is not meant to nullify other methods and interpretations but to enter into dialogue with those so that new meanings are produced and made relevant to other worlds and locations. This part of the sociorhetorical approach is important in two ways. First, it allows my Samoan world to be part of the interpretation and analysis of the text. Second, it affirms that my interpretation does not need to nullify traditional interpretations. It is not meant to impose the reader's location and situation on the text but to interact with the text, seeking how the text can answer one's questions. In this way, detailed attention is given to the text itself.

Two questions determine how I bring myself into the interpretive process. First, how does the sociorhetorical approach allow my world, represented by my hermeneutic of *tautuaileva*, to become part of the interpretive process? Second, when my world as a reader enters the process, how does a sociorhetorical approach deal with my interaction with the text?

The answer to the first question lies in what "sociorhetorical" means. Robbins explained that "socio" indicates the anthropological and sociological factors and characteristics of sociorhetorical criticism such as "social class, social systems, personal and community status, people on the margins, and people in position of power."[33] And "rhetorical" defines how the language in a text is used as a tool of communication.[34] Simply put, the sociorhetorical approach explores how language reflects and communicates the influences of social and cultural values and beliefs on the lives of people (no matter their faith commitments). It is these values and beliefs that I will analyse from my hermeneutic of *tautuaileva*.

---

[30] Robbins, *Exploring the Texture*, 1–2. See also Elaine M. Wainwright explained this combination in her article, "Reading Matthew 3–4: Jesus—Sage, Seer, Sophia, Son of God," *JSNT* 77 (2000): 28–29.

[31] Robbins, *Exploring the Texture of Texts,* 1.

[32] Robbins, *The Invention of Christian Discourse*, 5: "a socio-rhetorical interpretive analytic applies a politics of invitation, with a presupposition that the people invited into the conversation will contribute significantly new insights as a result of their particular experiences, identities, and concerns. In other words, a socio-rhetorical interpretive analytic presupposes genuine team work: people from different locations and identities working together with different cognitive frames for the purpose of getting as much insight as possible on the relation of things to one another."

[33] Robbins, *Exploring of Texture of Texts,* 1.

[34] Ibid., 1.

The answer to my second question is made evident in Robbins's diagram of the "socio-rhetorical model of textual communication:"[35]

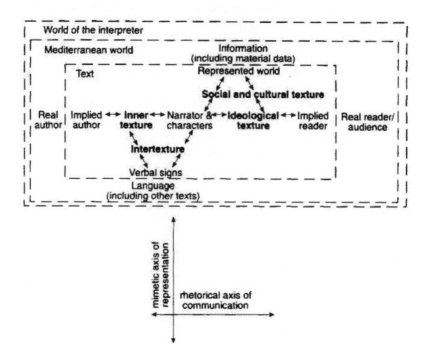

In the interaction between the reader and the text, the outside rectangle represents the world of the reader. This world is the location for the interaction of the reader's personal life and times with "the historical, social, cultural, ideological and religious worlds (encoded in the text)."[36] It is a world constructed of diverse ideologies. There are boundaries that divide the worlds of the interpreter, the text, and the author, but these boundaries are represented by broken lines which allow the interactions between those worlds, letting the meaning of the text and the effects of that meaning travel between them.[37]

These broken lines allow interaction between my Samoan world, about serving the needs of local family members in fa'aSamoa, and the Christian teachings about discipleship to travel to and from the world encoded in the Matthean text. In this way, sociorhetorical criticism facilitates how I in the Samoan

---

[35] See Vernon K. Robbins, *The Tapestry of Early Christian Discourse: Rhetoric, Society and Ideology* (New York: Routledge, 1996), 21.
[36] Ibid., 24.
[37] Ibid., 22.

world, with the tensions in its egalitarian and marginalizing cultures, might read the world encoded in the Matthean text. More importantly, it provides a way to explore marginality in the world of the Matthean author as it is encoded in the text.

Sociorhetorical criticism offers a framework that can facilitate a consideration of the needs of local family members in the text. This will bring my Samoan world into dialogue with the selected texts toward producing another interpretation of discipleship alongside the traditional interpretations.[38] Even though there are five stages in Robbins's sociorhetorical method, I will draw upon three of his stages—innertextual, intertextual, social/cultural—in this study to raise the hermeneutical questions that guide my *tautuaileva* readings of Matt 4:12–25 and 7:24–8:22.[39]

First, according to Robbins, innertextual analysis explores the text's use of "word patterns, voices, structures, devices, and modes in the text."[40] For this study, I will explore whether and how the language, narrative, and progressive textures of Matt 4:12–25 and Matt 7:24–8:22 (as rhetorical and narrative units that tell and show Jesus's ministry in Galilee) give attention to the needs, rights, and roles of the local people.

Second, Robbins describes intertextual analysis as showing how "the interpreter works in the area between the implied author and the text, not between the text and the reader." I will thus look at how other phenomena (from outside the text) speak through Matt 4:12–25 and Matt 7:24–8:22 to reveal Jesus's relationship to the crowd as showing other characteristics of discipleship.

Third, the Matthean text encodes a social and cultural context. Here the reading focuses on the text's "social and cultural nature *as* a text."[41] I will thus examine echoes in the text of first century Christians who experienced hardship and oppression under Roman imperial power. The text encodes the world of Christians and it is widely accepted that the Mediterranean world is the context of Matthew's community. Therefore, the social and cultural values of Matthew's community in the Mediterranean world will be reflected in this text.[42] It is not the purpose of a sociorhetorical approach to provide a thorough discussion of

---

[38] Ibid., 11.

[39] The other two stages are ideological texture and sacred texture.

[40] Robbins, *Exploring the Texture of Texts*, 7.

[41] Ibid., 71.

[42] Bruce J. Malina, "Understanding New Testament Persons," in *The Social Sciences and New Testament Interpretation*, ed. Richard Rohrbaugh (Peabody: Hendrickson, 1996), 42–43. To be fair to the New Testament writers, Malina suggests that it is important to understand how they understood people in their own world. This study assumes that the Matthean text was written in the first century Mediterranean world in the time of the Roman Empire.

Matthew's community and its historical, social and cultural values.[43] Rather, it focuses on the social and cultural textures embedded in the rhetoric of the texts which will advance the *tautuaileva* readings proposed in this study.

Postcolonial Approaches

Postcolonialism as a scholarly discipline is a consequence of, and a response to, colonialism. As a field of study, postcolonialism is "located within the wider concept of 'postcoloniality' and will be seen as the academic response to post-coloniality."[44] The term postcoloniality defines the postcolonial phenomenon as a discussion of the beginning and consequences of colonization, and reactions to that colonization. It is important to bear in mind that it is not possible to identify the starting point of postcoloniality. The definition of postcoloniality depends to a certain extent on the country and historical period under discussion. For example, my use of postcoloniality in relation to Samoa is twofold. First, it defines the influence of European colonization on Samoa, beginning from the eighteenth century. This colonial influence, nonetheless, includes missionaries' teachings. Second, it designates the internal colonization of the Samoan people by Samoans' own social and cultural practices and values.

The term postcolonialism is grounded in the history of European colonialist and institutional practices.[45] It has been used to examine reactions to European colonialism. It also designates a post-independence period—a time after a colonial power has formally withdrawn from a nation. From the late 1970s, the term postcolonialism has been utilised by literary and cultural studies scholars to discuss the cultural impact of colonization. It was an attempt to bring a political flavour into other fields of literary studies. Postcolonialism, like poststructuralism and postmodernism, is categorized and defined as a field of study that emerged after modernism.

---

[43] For details regarding the existence of Matthew's community in the Roman Empire and its system see Warren Carter, *Matthew and Empire: Initial Explorations* (Harrisburg: Trinity Press International, 2001), 9–53; Robert H. Gundry, "A Responsive Evaluation of the Social History of the Matthean Community in Roman Syria," in *Social History of the Matthean Community: Cross-Disciplinary Approaches*, ed. David L. Balch (Minneapolis: Fortress, 1991), 189–200; L. Michael White, "Crisis Management and Boundary Maintenance: The Social Location of the Matthean Community," in *Social History of the Matthean Community: Cross-Disciplinary Approaches*, ed. David L. Balch (Minneapolis: Fortress, 1991), 211–47.

[44] Anna Runesson, *Exegesis in the Making: Postcolonialism and New Testament Studies* (Leiden: Brill, 2011), 25.

[45] Bill Ashcroft, et al., *Post-Colonial Studies: The Key Concepts* (London: Routledge, 2000), 186–92.

The prefix "post" is a point of debate amongst scholars. To what does the "post" in postcolonialism refer? The difference between post-colonialism and postcolonialism provides an answer to this question. The hyphen incorporates two distinctively defined times, colonialism and after colonialism, as historical periods that seem to have no crossover. Without the hyphen, postcolonialism is a dynamic period—a historical period full of changes.[46] Homi Bhabha prefers this second sense of postcolonialism, accentuating the prefix "post" as indicating and expressing what he calls "beyond."[47] According to Bhabha, "post" meaning "beyond" defines the reality of the complex interdependent relationship between the colonizer and the colonized. It is Bhabha's definition of postcolonialism that I adopt in this study.

In the development of postcolonialism as a scholarly discipline, three scholars are key: Edward Said, Gayatri Spivak and Homi Bhabha. Their works are important in the development of my *tautuaileva* hermeneutic. Postcolonialism as a field of study appeared in literary and cultural studies when Edward Said's *Orientalism* came out in 1978 condemning western depictions of the Orient.[48] This work is based on Michael Foucault's notion of knowledge and power being used to accentuate the existence of imperialism and the resistance to it. According to Said, Europeans, by formalizing the study of the Orient and its representation in other literary and cultural texts such as novels and travel diaries, asserted particular ways of thinking which continue to drive and reinscribe the colonization of the Orient. Said argues that those colonial discourses show the construction of Europe as the dominant "self" (power) and the colonized Orient as the "other." His analysis is based on the notion of binary opposition between the "self" as colonizer and the "other" as the colonized. Said relates his exploration to biblical studies by requesting a postcolonial analysis of the Europeans' and Americans' discursive methods used in their interpretations of the Bible.

Spivak and Bhabha were critical of Said's colonial discourse analysis, particularly the notion of binary opposition. In her essay "Can the Subaltern Speak?" Spivak talks of difficulties of recovering the voices constructed in colonial texts, such as the voices of women.[49] According to Spivak, speaking should not be taken literally as talk. Women and natives did speak, but the problem was that there was already a constructed mindset in which the utterances of

---

[46] Ashcroft, et al., *Post-Colonial Studies*, 186–88.

[47] Homi Bhabha, *The Location of Culture* (London: Routledge, 1994), 1, 6, 26.

[48] Edward Said, *Orientalism: Western Conceptions of the Orient* (London: Penguin Books, 1978).

[49] Gayatri C. Spivak, "Can the Subaltern Speak?" in *Marxism and the Interpretation of Culture*, ed. Cary Nelson and Lawrence Grossberg (Urbana: University of Illinois Press, 1988), 271–314.

women and natives were historically categorized. In this way, an analysis of the voices in the notion of binary opposition continues to consider the voices of women and natives within that constructed type of thinking. However, native cultures are ripped apart by invasion and colonization by outsiders. Therefore, it is only from a shattering of "in-between" space that the women and natives can speak.

Bhabha argues that there is no fixed binary opposition between the colonizer and the colonized because both are caught in a complicated interdependent relationship. Given the complexity in their reciprocal relationship, it is important to explore what the results are of the crossing over of the colonizer's and colonized's cultures and how colonialism influenced those results. Bhabha is especially critical of Said's undermining of the ambivalent expression of colonial discourse when read and interpreted from the point of view of the colonized. Said's and Spivak's insights help make postcolonialism a reading strategy and Bhabha's work contributes toward making postcolonialism a state or condition of the reader.[50] The relevance of Bhabha's argument to the current study will be explored below.

Despite the formal withdrawal of colonial powers, colonialism exists in other forms and shapes in the so-called independent nations. For example, in terms of literary and cultural studies, although the colonial powers have left, their literature and interpretations continue to impact and influence the education of new generations in the former colonized nations, such as the conservative approach in theological schools in Samoa which uphold western traditional methods and interpretations of the Bible. Postcolonialism, as an academic reaction to that consequence, explores diverse colonial and postcolonial situations, responses and interactions as shown in different scholarly approaches such as liberation theology,[51] subaltern studies[52] and postcolonial feminist studies[53] that challenge those traditional methods.

Postcolonial Biblical Criticism

Postcolonial biblical criticism exposes the ways in which European powers used the Bible to legitimise colonial expansion.[54] It re-examines the texts, histories and cultures of the peoples that were changed by colonization.[55]

---

[50] R. S. Sugirtharajah, "A Postcolonial Exploration of Collusion and Construction in Biblical Interpretation," in *The Postcolonial Bible (Bible and Postcolonialism)*, ed. R. S. Sugirtharajah (Sheffield: Sheffield Academic, 1998), 93.

[51] See, e.g., Sugirtharajah, *Postcolonial Criticism*, 103–26.

[52] See, e.g., Guha Ranajit, ed., *A Subaltern Studies Reader, 1986–1995* (Minneapolis: University of Minnesota Press, 1997).

[53] See, e.g., Dube, *Postcolonial Feminist Interpretation*.

[54] Sugirtharajah, *Postcolonial Criticism and Biblical Interpretation*, 43–44.

The Bible is literature comprised of colonial and postcolonial histories, stories, and theologies. Considering the New Testament as (a) construction(s) and invention(s) of first century Christians,[56] it consists of texts produced by authors and received by readers who were historically and socially conditioned.[57] These constructions and inventions were influenced by colonial and postcolonial societies. For example, first century Mediterranean society was a colonial society under Roman imperial rule. This same society can also be considered a postcolonial society because it continued to be influenced by the Hellenistic world of Alexander the Great, until the Roman Empire established its control around the Mediterranean. Thus, because New Testament histories, stories and messages came out of the first century Mediterranean world, the effects and consequences of that colonial/postcolonial time and space are reflected in the New Testament literature.

Segovia uses the intercultural study approach to explore colonial and postcolonial issues in the biblical text. He retrieves unheard voices in the text, opens up spaces to make these voices recognized, examines power relations and their influences which oppress these voices in the text, and considers how these relations define the cultural situations of certain readers.[58] Regarding the application of postcolonialism in studies of Matthew, Mark Allan Powell writes:

> in studies of Matthew, postcolonial critics seek to recover "silenced voices" in the history and culture of Gospel interpretation and in the Gospel itself. The process of doing this often involves contesting presuppositions and either exposing or accentuating the political implications of dominant interpretations of the Gospel. For example, postcolonial critics seek to articulate the view that Matthew's Gospel takes toward imperial power (the Roman Empire) and toward those who were subordinated and dominated by that power.[59]

Postcolonialism's applicability to my study of Matthew's perspective revolves around discipleship and family ties and their interpretations. This study is

---

[55] Ibid.,11.

[56] See Vernon K. Robbins, *The Invention of Christian Discourse*, vol. 1 (Blandform Forum: Deo, 2009), 21.

[57] Fernando S. Segovia, "Toward Interculturalism: Reading Strategy from the Diaspora," in *Reading from This Place: Social Location and Biblical Interpretation in Global Perspective*, ed. Fernando F. Segovia and Mary Ann Tolbert, vol. 2 (Minneapolis: Fortress, 1995), 321–30.

[58] Fernando F. Segovia, "Postcolonial Criticism and the Gospel of Matthew," in *Methods of Matthew*, ed. Mark Allan Powell (Cambridge: Cambridge University Press, 2009), 207.

[59] Mark Allan Powell, "Introduction," in *Methods of Matthew*, ed. Mark Allan Powell (Cambridge: Cambridge University Press, 2009), 10.

an exploration of power relations in the world encoded in the text, and of Matthew's account of Jesus's ministry dealing with the needs of local people in local contexts ruled and controlled by Roman imperial power and by other colonial systems. Thus, in this study, postcolonialism provides a lens on how Matthean narrator of Jesus's ministry tells and shows the ambivalence of the crowds as the colonized, and how they seek survival in the Roman imperial, Jewish religious, and Mediterranean social and cultural colonial worlds. While there are a number of elements to postcolonial readings,[60] I will concentrate on the concept of hybridity as third space.

Hybridity as Third Space for Service

One of the analytical tools of postcolonial thinking is Homi Bhabha's concept of hybridity. This concept emphasizes cross-cultural reading but goes beyond intercultural criticism because it recognizes the complexities in the interdependent relationship between the colonized and the colonizer. It is a transcultural approach which allows the marginalized or colonized situation of a reader to become a key to an interpretation of the Bible. It does not impose that situation on the text, but rather provides a departure point for seeking in the text an understanding that would define a transformation of that situation.

Bhabha defines hybridity as a mixture of identity or culture in a "third space" in which colonized people respond to colonial rule.[61] He writes:

> these "in-between" spaces provide the terrain for elaborating strategies of selfhood—singular or communal—that initiate new signs of identity, and innovative sites of collaboration, and contestation, in the act of defining the idea of society itself.[62]

Hybridity is an in-between space in which different cultures and identities meet.[63] It is the space at which the relationship between the colonized and the

---

[60] Other important postcolonial concepts include nativist, resistance and intercultural optics. First, the nativist approach is a reading strategy that allows an indigenous people's pre-colonial and colonial histories, cultures and contexts to inform their reading practice. Second, postcolonialism is also "a resistant discourse, which tries to write back and work against colonial assumptions, representation, and ideologies" (R. S. Sugirtharajah, *Asian Biblical Hermeneutics and Postcolonialism: Contesting Interpretation* [Sheffield: Sheffield Academic, 1998], ix, x). And third, the intercultural (cross-cultural) approach emerged from the diaspora experience. Its leading advocate is Fernando Segovia (See Segovia, "Toward Interculturalism," 321–30).

[61] Bhabha, *The Location of Culture*, 163.

[62] Ibid., 2.

[63] Hybridity will be clarified by two terms that make up this model. First, the term *mimicry* describes the ambivalent relationship between the colonizer and the colonized in

colonizer takes place. It is a borderland space. This space is characterized by resistance and conflict. In this study, hybridity is used to identify my location as an interpreter in the Samoan society. I place myself in the borderland space seeking an opportunity to survive as a member of the Samoan world.[64]

Discussing hybridity as a mixture of identity or culture has its limitations. Robert Young, for instance, suggests that hybridity has prejudiced roots because it is grounded in the racially-biased discourse of nineteenth century evolutionary theory.[65] Paul Gilroy similarly argues that it disregards the importance of pure parents giving attention to impure offspring.[66] Steven Engler sees as another weakness of hybridity the overemphasis of differences in time and space due to the accentuating of historical origins over what is really happening. Engler adds that this differentiation can be misleading when a particular tradition or way of thinking at a certain time and space is used in a way that could bring about misleading or invented traditions and ideologies.[67] John Hutnyk offers another criticism of hybridity, arguing that it underemphasizes existing differences by drawing attention to apparent distinctions while ignoring the important hidden ones. According to Hutnyk, hybridity overlooks serious differences and assumes equality where important issues are concealed, such as power and authority.[68]

The concept of hybridity identifies and describes something that is not pure. From the point of view of those seeking survival, the weaknesses of using "hybridity" as a postcolonial approach—its biased roots, impure offspring, overemphasis and underemphasis of distinctions in different times and space— points to the importance of what hybridity really means. These are the complexi-

---

colonial and postcolonial discourse (see Ashcroft et al., *Post-Colonial Studies*, 139). Second, the term *ambivalence* describes a persistent fluctuation which occurs through wanting one thing and its opposite at the same time (see Bhabha, *The Location of Culture*, 121–31, 145–74).

[64] On what "borderland" as space means in defining location of an individual or a group, see Ken A. Grant, "Living in the Borderlands—An An Identity and a Proposal," *Di* 49.1 (2010): 26–33; S.N.J.M. Sophia Park, "The Galilean Jesus: Creating a Borderland at the Foot of the Cross (Jn 19:23–30)," *TS* 70 (2009): 419–36; Sherry B. Ortner, "Borderland Politics and Erotics: Gender and Sexuality in Himalayan Mountaineering," in *Making Gender: The Politics and Erotics of Culture* (Boston: Beacon, 1996), 181–212; Elaine M. Wainwright, *Women Healing/Healing Women: The Genderization of Healing in Early Christianity* (London: Equinox, 2006), 17–18, 143–46.

[65] Robert Young, *Colonial Desire: Hybridity in Theory, Culture and Race* (London: Routledge, 1995), 6–19.

[66] Paul Gilroy, *Between Camps: Nations, Cultures and The Allure of Race* (London: Routledge, 2004), 105–06, 117, 250–51.

[67] Steven Engler, "Tradition's Legacy" in *Historicizing Tradition in the Study of Religion*, ed. Steven Engler and Gregory P. Grieve (New York: deGruyter, 2005), 357–78.

[68] John Hutnyk, "Hybridity," *ERS* 28 (2005): 96–99.

ties of the reciprocal relationships that people are engaged in at different levels as a result of colonisation. Hybridity represents the unpredictability of what is happening to a reader in a particular situation, which is no different from what Doreen Massey called "places and their identities (that are) always unfixed, contested and multiple."[69] That unpredictability asserts what Bhabha describes as *ambivalence* in the complex relationship between the colonizer and the colonized. In other words, the unpredictability represented by hybridity reflects the ability of the people to act and respond to any situation on the spot according to their own needs.

Sometimes the weighing up of mixtures of understandings, cultures and values can be unbalanced and misleading; but no hybridity is balanced. For example, in my case, I was born in Samoa but most of my education was done in Aotearoa New Zealand.[70] In that complex, I am a hybrid myself. When making decisions as a family member of a Samoan family in Aotearoa New Zealand, this unbalanced and unfixed situation has many ramifications. It may mean a swing toward the Aotearoa New Zealand way of life which could affect the Samoan way of thinking, or vice versa. Despite this fluctuation between two cultural spaces there will be a positive outcome—survival in the dominant culture.

The complexity of in-between spaces produces a positive outcome beneficial to the person in that situation. It is an opportunity to go beyond the boundaries that have held back a marginalized, ambivalent and confused person from seeking ways that will help him or her survive in a particular place.

I utilise the postcolonial concept of hybridity to define the space and location in which I place myself as a Samoan reader. Choosing hybridity enables the disciples (*tautua*) in my world and in the world of the Matthean text to respond to the colonial rule in my world, in the text, and in its history of interpretation.

Conclusion

This chapter has shown that interpretations of discipleship are influenced by the methods used by interpreters. While the traditional methods tend to dominate scholarship, their interpretations have focussed on certain aspects of discipleship to the neglect of others. I maintain that the consideration of discipleship in a particular local place in the Matthean story, which has been overlooked by the global-orientation of traditional methods, needs attention.

The methods that approach the text from the world of the reader enable a richer exploration of discipleship in the Matthean text. Such methods draw attention to the needs of local people, families and communities in the local world

---

[69] Doreen Massey, *Space, Place and Gender* (Cambridge: Polity, 1994), 5.
[70] My use of Aotearoa New Zealand reflects the hybridity concept that leads to the *tautuaileva* (service in-between spaces) hermeneutics used in this study.

encoded in the Matthean text. There are parts of the Matthean story that show Jesus's summoning followers to return and help their families, such as the sending of the centurion back to his household (Matt 5:5–13).

My approach is influenced by my sense of identity and understanding of my place in the Samoan social and cultural world. That sense of place is determined by my experience of social, cultural, economic, and religious issues, and my understanding of how people relate to one another in Samoan culture. The key issue that shapes this study is the failure of the understanding and practice of traditional discipleship to account for the needs and rights of local people. That issue evokes for me egalitarianism as the critical element to expose the marginalized in my world, and in the text.

Who I am as a Samoan is not static. As such, I employ the postcolonial concept of hybridity in order to account for the complex and unique way in which my identity functions. My use of the postcolonial approach is intended to identify my location as a reader and to inform my analysis of discipleship in the Matthean text. It signifies who I was/am as Samoan: someone who was marginalized and colonized but is now realizing a way to approach life in today's world. It is where other cultures and values are accepted as important because they have embodied opportunities that help me survive. It allows my local situation as a reader to be defined and analysed within the global importance of God's message of salvation.[71] It appropriates the ideology of survival underlying my reading. The postcolonial concept of hybridity enables me to identify the expression and structures of the negotiated interdependent relationships between colonizer and colonized in my context and in the text. It also reveals colonized subjects surviving in the text, and points to the possibility of colonized subjects surviving in my context.

---

[71] This is different from the intercultural criticism approach which does not consider marginalization and oppression as a key to interpreting the Bible.

2.

TAUTUA (SERVICE) AT THIRD SPACE

This chapter explains my location in third space which I develop into the *tautuaileva* (service in-between spaces) hermeneutics in the next chapter. Entrance into this third space is determined by my place as *tautua* (servant) in a Samoan family, church and society. *Tautua* is not about status. Rather, it is a family- and community-based social and cultural role. Being *tautua* exhibits my role and responsibility to my family and church regardless of my gender, academic achievements or status as a father and a minister in the church.

The following exploration begins by defining the concepts of "identity" and "place" from cultural and ethnic perspectives, followed by my explanation of how *tautua* shapes that perspective. Part of my concerns as *tautua* is to identify problems that hamper the fulfillment of my roles and thus to find ways to overcome those problems. In the third section, I identify the problems that determine how I enter the third space. The overriding problems are marginalization and inequality, which are exacerbated by the traditional teachings of discipleship in Samoan society. The chapter concludes by specifying the categories of my location that will be utilised as hermeneutical lenses in the interpretation of the Matthean texts.

Identity and Place

According to the *Oxford English Dictionary*, identity is "the quality or condition of being the same substance, composition, nature, properties, or in particular qualities under consideration; absolute or essential sameness; oneness."[1] Identity defines how I am the same as, and distinct from, other Samoans. I am thus to be identified in accordance with my individual characteristics and in regard to the characteristics of a group of people to which I belong.

I focus on my social and cultural identity as Samoan, with the understanding that Samoa is a local place with its own cultures, values, spaces and people. The Samoan social and cultural world provides the lens which informs my seeing, experiencing, and exploring of everyday life. To introduce what identity means to me as a Samoan, I use the character of being a servant in the Samoan culture of service (*tautua*). The *tautua* listens, sees, and feels the needs of his or her family and village, and acts to fulfill them despite challenges. Identity is not just about identifying a person according to the culture to which s/he belongs,

---

[1] *Oxford English Dictionary*, online, s.v. "Identity."

but also how s/he puts that culture into action. Identity is action-in-progress that is persistently shaped by the changes one encounters in the world(s) in which s/he lives. In this way, my sense of identity as *tautua* is dynamic.

Identity cannot be fully understood without a sense of place, or "a particular point on earth's surface; an identifiable location for a situation imbued with human values."[2] Place is not just a location. It is also a space identified by various situations emergent from interactions among people with their values. In this regard, place is a location lived and controlled by people. It is where I learn how to live and relate to other people. It is also the environment where I experience (un)familiar situations based on the human values accepted by people who inhabit that place. In this way, understanding the particular place to which I belong in a society determines how I see and experience other places. More importantly, it shapes how I see other people in other places. Thus, a sense of place is important in defining who I am as a Samoan.

Tautua Identity and Place

According to Charles Taylor "we cannot understand another society until we have understood ourselves better as well."[3] For me, in order to understand discipleship as a service that aims to help those in need, I have to understand the culture of service (*tautua*) in my Samoan world. The culture of *tautua* is a family-based social and cultural role, value and practice, that views the needs, rights and roles of people in the family and community as primary. I am immersed in and through that culture as a *tautua*. It is the *fatuaiga tausi* (role of a member of the family) of any member of a Samoan family regardless of status and gender. Thus, the fundamental existence of *tautua* begins within the family.

Tautua *as Concept*

Tautua is made up of two syllables: *tau* and *tua*. The definitions of the word *tau* as a verb are "relate, reach, fight, read or count" and as a noun it means "coverings of an *umu*, and weather." The first syllable *tau* describes the undertaking of the *tautua* as a reaching-out to serve the family. The word *tua* refers to the back of a body, and it also designates the back space (as opposed to the front) where the service of *tautua* is undertaken. *Tua* emphasizes the back of the *tautua's* body that will carry out the tasks required of the *tautua* role, despite their weight and difficulty.

---

[2] Susan Mayhew, *A Dictionary of Geography* (Oxford: Oxford University Press, 1997), 327.

[3] Charles Taylor, *Philosophy and the Human Sciences: Philosophical Papers* (Cambridge: Cambridge University Press, 1985), 129.

The role of *tautua* is understood in relation to the *matai* as head of the family and how that role is undertaken. The second syllable *tua* acknowledges the social and cultural spaces in *fa'aSamoa* where the *tautua* roles are to be undertaken—the back place opposite the front place where the *matai* sits and dwells. When the *tautua* keeps to the back place in serving the *matai* and the family, this is considered as *tautua tausi-va, e iloa le va fealoa'i* (a service that respects the space between members of the family). Because *tua* is the place where *tautua* carries out her/his role, it is also regarded as her/his residing place. S/he builds a Samoan house (*fale*) behind the family house where s/he keeps the equipment needed to fulfill the *tautua* role.

The *tautua* also comes "behind" the family in terms of when s/he takes her/his turn to eat, talk, and rest. The *tautua* puts the parents and family, especially the young siblings, ahead of her/himself. The *tautua* prepares and serves food to the family and at meal times, s/he sits at the back and waits until the family are satisfied. The left-over food will be her/his meal. But if there is none left, s/he will not eat. As a *tautua*, s/he does not worry about her/his stomach as long as the family are satisfied. The way s/he serves the parents makes them happy because it is a sign of the *tautua* becoming a good family leader in the future. For the siblings, how s/he fulfills *tautua* role will be a good example for them to follow.

Tautua plays out in two important places.[4] First, it identifies the role of the untitled men in the Samoan *matai* system. Second, it expresses the value of serving the family.

Tautua *as Sense of Place*

My identity as *tautua* is expressed in Samoan as *fa'asinomaga*.[5] This word is made up of *fa'asino* and *maga*.[6] *Fa'asino* is a verb meaning "point" or "direct," which points a Samoan to a particular family and village to which s/he belongs or is linked.[7] *Fa'asino* refers to the families and villages to which a *tautua* belongs, holds title names, customary lands, and residential places. The second

---

[4] See Ama'amalele Tofaeono, *Eco-Theology: Aiga The Household of Life; A Perspective from Living Myths and Traditions* (Erlangen: Erlangen Verlag für Mission Und Okumene, 2000), 300; G. B. Milner, *Samoan Dictionary: Samoan-English, English-Samoan* (Oxford: Oxford University Press, 1966), 245–48.

[5] There is a saying in Samoan, *O le tagata ma lona fa'asinomaga* (the person and his or her sense of identity), which expresses the connection a person has to a particular family.

[6] Martin Mariota's definition of *faasinomaga* considers *maga* to be the "point where a road splits into two or more different roads" (Martin W. Mariota, "A Samoan *Palagi* Reading of Exodus 2–3" [MTh Thesis, University of Auckland, 2012], 50). However, the *maga* in *fa'asinomaga* is a suffix that transforms a verb into a noun (as I explain above).

[7] Milner, *Samoan Dictionary*, 50.

part, *maga*, is a suffix[8] that makes *fa'asino* a noun, *fa'asinomaga*. Thus, *fa'asinomaga* identifies a *tautua* in and through his or her social and cultural links to a Samoan family and village. *Fa'asinomaga* points a *tautua* to his/her social and cultural role. S/he belongs to a particular family structure within the Samoan *matai* system.[9] The hierarchy of *matai* titles[10] is made in accordance with the recognition of a *matai* title in the honorific address of each family,[11] village, church, district, and in Samoa as a nation. The *matai* system is accepted by Samoan people as the central part of their social and cultural traditions. The

---

[8] Ibid.,120.

[9] In Samoan customs, the family to which a person belongs is identified and considered in accordance with how the chiefly title of that family is recognized in the village and at district and national levels. A Samoan is placed in a social and cultural system known as the *matai* system. The *matai* system runs in the family, village, district and national levels. At each level, certain layers of the *matai* system are identified. People on each layer have roles which define how they relate to each other. For example, at the family level, there are three layers of the *matai* system. On the first layer are the *matai* title holders. The second layer is women and children, and the third layer is the untitled men. Each *matai* (*ali'i* or *tulafale*) has his own categorization in connection with a recognized honorific address acceptable to a family, village, district, and national levels (See Saleimoa Vaai, *Samoa Faamatai and the Rule of Law* [Apia: National University of Samoa Press, 1999], 29–30). Through this categorization, chiefs of paramount status are distinguished from chiefs of lesser importance in national gatherings. See, Lealaiauloto Nofoaiga Kitiona and Fuataga L. Tauiliili, *O le Faavae o Samoa Anamua* (Apia: Malua Printing Press, 1985), 8.

[10] There are two types of *matai:* the *al'ii* (high chief) and the *tulafale* (orator or talking chief) with *ali'i* as the paramount of the two. The *ali'i* is treated with great respect in family and village events. The *tulafale* has his own roles such as making and delivering speeches. In any family or village activity, the *tulafale* will do the talking on behalf of the *ali'i* and the whole family. Thus *tulafale* are the orators or talking chiefs. Usually, the *ali'i* is chosen to be the head of an extended family.

Some villages and families however do not have *ali'i* titles, but only *tulafale* titles. In these cases, the most important *tulafale* is the head of the family. For example, the village of Faletagaloa Safune in Savaii does not have *ali'i*. This has no effect on how their village is ranked in the Safune District. Traditionally in this district, one of its villages, Lefagaoalii (simply translated as the Bay or the Seat of *Ali'i*) is where all the *ali'i*, including those who used to be seated as *ali'i* at Faletagaloa are now placed.

[11] At the family and village levels, each *matai* belongs to a residential place and area of land (*tulaga maota, tulaga laoa*) in the village, a customary place that belongs to a *matai* title. The *matai* elected by the family as a resident of this customary residence is the family head and is known by the term *Sa'o* (meaning "straight or true"). *Sa'o* as a family leader is expected to be the decision-maker, in the right way. *Sa'o* is a *matai* at the top of the family system. The last group in rank is the untitled men, the *tautua*. *Tautua* is not a place of oppression but a place of seeking knowledge and understanding, of living life as a member of the family.

tautua is positioned at the lowest rank of the *matai* system. This does not mean that the *tautua* is not important but that s/he will face challenges in providing food and security for the (extended) family. This is why *tautua* is called *malosi o le aiga ma le nuu* (the strength of the family and village).

Fa'asinomaga (sense of belonging to a place) of a *tautua* points to particular relationships in the family and certain roles to carry out. Examples of those relationships are the *tautua's* relationship to the *matai* and to his sisters.[12] Carrying out his role in those relationships is demonstrated by the Samoan word *va fealoa'i*. *Va* refers to space (actual and metaphorical) between people and social, cultural and religious systems. This space is relational. The word *fealoa'i* means to interact respectfully. Thus, *va fealoa'i* designates respectful relationships in-between people, and between people and the social and cultural systems in the society. *Tautua* is thus expected to relate to other people and spaces with respect.

These spaces are relational and have boundaries described in Samoan as *tuaoi*. *Tuaoi* is the short form of the Samoan phrase *tua atu o i* which means "beyond this point."[13] It expresses the expectation that respect is given to other people, who own customary lands, and who hold social and cultural status in the *matai* system. The function of *tuaoi* is not to separate the person in high status as colonizer from the person in the low status as colonized. Rather, *tuaoi* reveals the importance of the social and cultural order in a local Samoan family and community where the young people respect the elders and where untitled men and women respect the person chosen by the family as family leader.

A *tautua's* sense of place as *fa'asinomaga* concerns how s/he is linked to her/his family and the space of her/his family in the village. Part of that

---

[12] The sharing of the *tautua* role is the essence of the sister-brother relationship in *fa'aSamoa*. This relationship teaches the sister and brother their roles, in the interest of the family and the community. For example, the sister learns to be a craftsperson, a priest, a peacemaker, a healer, a teacher, a chief and a saviour (see Aiono F. Le Tagaloa, *O le Faasinomaga: Le Tagata ma lona Faasinomaga* [Alafua: Lamepa, 1997], 16–20). How she exercises her roles will bestow honor on her family in the community. As a craftsperson, she makes a variety of beautiful handicrafts. Their quality and quantity affect the rating of the wealth of her family. As a priest she conducts worship. (See Penelope Schoeffel, "The Samoan Concept of *Feagaiga* and its Transformation," in *Tonga and Samoa: Images of Gender and Polity*, ed. Judith Huntsman [Christchurch: University of Canterbury, 1995], 85–105.) Being a healer, she heals the sick. She has to teach family genealogies, traditions and myths. She is a chief and has her own post in the circle of the family's chiefs.

[13] See TuiAtua Tupua Tamasese Ta'isi Efi's "Keynote Address for Pacific Futures Law and Religion Symposium" (National University of Samoa, Lepapaigalagala, Samoa, 3 December 2008), accessed at http://www.head-of-state-samoa.ws/pages/welcome.html on 14 July 2013.

fa'asinomaga is the relationships to which s/he belongs and her/his role in those relationships.

A good *tautua* is called by other names such as *tautai* and *tufuga*. *Tautai* is given to a good fisherperson who despite rough seas and weather comes back with plenty of fish to feed the family. A *tufuga* has good skills in tattooing or building houses. In these regards, a good *tautua* is one whose actions speak louder than words hence the value given to *tautua-le-pa'o* or *tautua-le-pisa*, which means "to serve with silence." Silence from a *tautua* does not mean sub-mission to oppression but respect to a commitment to carry out a service role to the best of his ability, thus ensuring the survival of the family.[14] This initiative is exhibited in the Samoan phrase *loto fuatiaifo* which connotes the subjectivity required to initiate good relations and respect with regard to each other's needs and rights regardless of situation, status, gender, race, and colour.[15]

Loto fuatiaifo is made up of three words: *Loto* means a person's will; *fuatia* means hit or touch; *ifo* means bow. Putting the words together reveals subjec-tivity in the Samoan world as a feeling in which a person's heart is touched, producing an attraction which makes him or her deny self-needs. This reveals the emotional element that is important in undertaking *tautua* in the interests of others. The *tautua* faces challenges for the sake of the family with humility and respect. A *tautua* can still make his voice heard but in a respectful way.

My role as a *tautua* to my family and church opens my eyes to challenges faced by Samoan families and churches. One of these challenges is the inability to fulfill the demands of the church and family at the same time. For the church, the main challenge is criticism of the preaching and practicing of traditional discipleship that give primary attention to church needs. Understanding my role as *tautua* has opened my eyes to problems that hinder the undertaking of that role in the Samoan society. Identifying the problem that determines my entering the third space will be shown in a brief account and analysis of my journey as a *tautua*.

---

[14] Unfortunately, this essential undertaking of the *tautua* is abused by those in positions of power. Sometimes, chiefs treat *tautua* with oppressive ways when the *tautua* are dis-tant relatives or adopted members of the family.

[15] Jeannette M. Mageo describes subjectivity in the Samoan world in the following way: "In Samoa *loto* (will), 'subjectivity,' is the marginalized element of the self" (Jeannette Marie Mageo, *Theorizing Self in Samoa: Emotions, Genders, and Sexualities* [Michigan: The University of Michigan Press, 1998], 11). In my opinion, *loto fuatiaifo* fits her defi-nition of subjectivity.

Tautuaileva: **Service at In-between Spaces**

In my review of postcolonial approaches in chapter one, hybridity is an intervening space [16] which is not a new horizon but a location that Bhabha calls "beyond."[17] In this sense, hybridity is a third space which gives any person an opportunity to explore the text beyond the norms of the past and the present. Bhabha considered these intervening spaces because they are where minoritized and colonized subjects interrogate moments and processes brought about by "the articulation of cultural differences."[18] From the point of view of a colonized person,[19] hybridity is about occupying or returning to the present to discover signs of identity fruitful to one's life or future. Thus, hybridity is an appropriate in-between space to define my situation as reader and one that will be employed to explore discipleship in the Matthean text.

The norms of traditional discipleship that we have been taught, and have practiced in Samoa, contradict the inclusive nature of the culture of service in Samoan culture and in Jesus's vision of ἡ βασιλεία τῶν οὐρανῶν. Thus, I have decided to break away from the familiar spaces of family and church, that practiced traditional discipleship and gives primary attention to church needs, and to enter an unfamiliar space—the space where I will be critical of the traditional characteristics of discipleship and its practice in Samoan society.

---

[16] Bhabha claimed "hybridity intervenes in the exercise of authority not merely to indicate the impossibility of its identity but to represent the unpredictability of its presence" (Bhabha, *The Location of Culture*, 163).

[17] Ibid., 1–2.

[18] Ibid.,2.

[19] There are other studies by Samoan scholars that identify who they are in relation to family and church, including studies by Samoans borned and raised in New Zealand who are caught in-between cultures and understandings. Jemaima Tiatia in *Caught between Cultures: New Zealand-Born Pacific Island Perspective* (Ellerslie: Christian Research Association, 1998), describes her early twenties as a Samoan born raised in New Zealand. She stresses that New Zealand-born Samoans have unique experiences based on "the dual conflict between one's Island upbringing and the westernised or 'Europeanised' other self."

Risatisone Ete raises the same dilemma of being caught between the New Zealand *palagi* and Samoan worlds (Risatisone Ete, "Ugly Duckling, Quacking Swan," in *Faith in a Hyphen: Cross-Cultural Theologies Down Under*, ed. Clive Pearson and Jione Havea (Adelaide: Openbook Publishers, 2005), 43–48. Unlike Tiatia, Ete is not critical of the *fa'aSamoa* and the church. The hybrid of *palagi* and Samoan worlds is also seen in Ete's experience as a New Zealand born Samoan, who experiences a positive side to it. For Ete, hybridity is strengthening. See also Melanie Anae's study, "Fofoaivaoese" and Albert Wendt's novel *Sons for The Return Home* (Auckland: Penguin, 1973).

I enter this unfamiliar space in order to fulfill my role as a *tautua* to my family and church. I also seek to make sense of Jesus's ministry in that world. I call this third space, *tautuaileva* (service in-between spaces).

Tautuaileva is the word I coin as short form of the Samoan phrase *tautua i le va*. *Tautuaileva* refers to service carried out in-between spaces, as well as to a servant who stands in-between spaces. It expresses the expectation that service in a family or community is reciprocal and the needs and rights of everyone are important.

My use of *tautuaileva* as one word is symbolic. It shows my hybrid location as third space, at which there is no gap between my understanding of service in Samoan and in Christian cultures. It reveals that in times of undertaking my service role to both my family and church units, I negotiate and renegotiate the fulfillment of my needs and roles in relation to both units, depending on which unit's needs are given priority. It is the location where I stand as *tautua* allowing myself to accept changes and challenges in life that help me fulfill my role and responsibility to my family and church. As such, *tautua* is no longer restricted to a particular level, space, culture or people. A *tautua* needs courage to face challenges and changes in today's world such as the courage to break away from the expectations considered as traditions in his or her place of belonging and to seek other ways that will assist his or her *tautua*.

The third space of *tautuaileva* is a dynamic location where I move, as a *tautua*, to and from places and act in accordance with the reality of life in my everyday life as a Samoan. This is where I stand as a Samoan and from which I see life in today's world.

3.

TAUTUAILEVA AMONG ISLANDER APPROACHES

This chapter explains how my location in *tautuaileva* provides hermeneutical lenses to inform my analyses of the Matthean texts. The first section includes a brief review of studies by Samoan biblical scholars who design and utilise cultural hermeneutics in their readings of the Bible. This sets the scene for my appealing to Samoan cultural and social location in third space as a hermeneutic in this study. I will close the chapter by explaining how I fuse *tautuaileva* with sociorhetorical criticism as the interpretational tool to analyse the Matthean texts in part 2.

As indicated above, I present the *tautuaileva* hermeneutic as my contribution to the development of Islander criticism. I construct *tautuaileva* with Samoan ideas and languages, and I imagine and expect that biblical critics and readers of other islands in Oceania and beyond could appropriate and associate my constructions with similar ways and modes in their island contexts. Furthermore, I hope that non-islanders would be able to find something relevant in my study for their reading approaches and practices in their own contexts.

Samoan Approaches

Several Samoan scholars have contributed to and developed biblical and theological scholarship from our cultural perspectives. One of the problems in these studies is that the use of Samoan backgrounds is not always clearly stated and explained. Given the scope of this study, I am not able to review all the contributions to Samoan Hermeneutics.[1] Instead I will describe the recent studies by Mosese Mailo,[2] PeniLeota,[3] Frank Smith,[4] Arthur Wulf[5] and Martin Mariota,[6]

---

[1] Other studies include Fereti S. Panapa, "The Significance of Hospitality in the Traditions of the First Testament and its Parallels to the Samoan Culture of Talimalo" (MTh Thesis, University of Auckland, 2000); Faitala Talapusi, "Jesus Christ in the Pacific World of Spirits" (BD Thesis, Pacific Theological College, 1976); Fa'atauva'a Tapua'i, "A Comparative Study of the Samoan and Hebrew Concepts of the Covenant" (BD Thesis, Pacific Theological College, 1972).

[2] Mosese Mailo, *Bible-ing My Samoan: Native Language and the Politics of Bible Translating in the Nineteenth Century* (Apia: Piula Publications, 2016).

[3] Leota, "Ethnic Tensions in Persian-Period Yehud."

[4] Smith, "The Johannine Jesus from a Samoan perspective."

who describe how their Samoan experience and understanding are utilised as part of their reading strategies. Their approaches help situate and clarify how I understand *our* Samoan world, my location in hybridity, and how those shape my hermeneutical lens.

I start with Mosese Ma'ilo because it is different from other works dealt with below especially in emphasizing the use of postcolonial approaches (focusing on decolonization and emancipation) to investigate ideologies behind Bible translation in the nineteenth century. Ma'ilo, a biblical scholar, utilizes his expertise in the Samoan language, life, and culture in his investigation. Bible translation in the nineteenth century was done and controlled by the missionaries, and Ma'ilo's study exposes the colonial and controlling poetics embedded in these translations.

One example of Ma'ilo's attempt to decolonize Bible translation (to Samoan) is his chapter on Luke 15:11–32 which he entitles "Emancipating Luke 15:11–32 from mission."[7] He has a double concern: to emancipate the content of Luke 15:11–32 from the biased theologies of the missionary translators, and to emancipate the Samoan language from the control of the foreign missionary translators. While my study is not directly about bible translation, I am encouraged by Ma'ilo's critical work.

Peni Leota, an Old Testament scholar, engages in a cross-cultural study of the ethnic tensions in the texts of Ezra-Nehemiah and Chronicles and the issue of land tenure behind recent claims of maintaining native culture that are in conflict with human rights in the Samoan society. Leota's concerns relate to contemporary tensions between Samoan residents and migrants in defining identity in the Samoan society. He engages in an analogical interpretation of two different worlds which are socially and culturally based. Leota utilises cultural pluralism as a dialogical approach to engage the text. He approaches the text with questions, concerns, and interpretive frameworks and then enters into a reading process. Leota as reader has in mind the experience and understanding of his own world, socially, culturally and politically. The engagement between reader and text evokes for Leota questions that shape an interpretation of the text and of his Samoan world.

Leota's work depends on the plurality of cultures while acknowledging the distance between the Samoan world and the world behind the text of Ezra-Nehemiah and Chronicles. Leota's analogical approach however does not consider marginalization and oppression as key to biblical interpretation. Nor does he consider the influence of the social, cultural, and economic systems on the

---

[5] Arthur John Wulf, "Was Earth Created Good? Reappraising Earth in Genesis 1:1–2:4a from a Samoan *Gafataulima* Perspective" (PhD Thesis, University of Auckland, 2016).

[6] Mariota, "A Samoan *Palagi* Reading of Exodus 2–3," ix, 1–5.

[7] Mailo, *Bible-ing My Samoan*, 263–65.

life situation of a reader in the reading process. These matters, on the other hand, make a difference in my *tautuaileva* reading.

Frank Smith, a New Testament scholar, studies Jesus in John's Gospel from a Samoan perspective. Like Leota, Smith utilises the analogical approach. For Smith, one of the problems that one encounters as a Samoan reader of the Fourth Gospel is that the world of John is different from the Samoan social and cultural world. Smith develops a way to bring these two worlds together. He draws on his experience and understanding of the Samoan social and cultural world, and makes an analogical interpretation of cultural values and practices in certain parts of the text.

Smith's use of the analogical approach exhibits a similar weakness to Leota's study. With his Samoan experience and worldviews in his intercultural study, he acknowledges the distance between texts, readers and their experiences. His intercultural approach does not consider colonization and oppression as key to biblical interpretation. Smith's study is more about comparing readings and ideologies which are socially and culturally based. Thus, the impact of the social, cultural and economic systems on the life situation of a reader is not properly accounted for in his reading process.

Arthur Wulf, an Old Testament scholar, in his study of Gen 1:1–2:4a, presents a reading of the creation stories from a Samoan ecological approach called *gafataulima* (accomplish, fulfil, capable). Wulf wrote that his inspiration to this study arose out of a personal experience with natural disasters in his Samoan local context. This experience contradicts his understanding of the perfect image of God's creation in the book of Genesis which raises the question: Was Earth created good?

Wulf's use of a Samoan perspective is similar to Ma'ilo. They both acknowledge the colonized in their locations as readers, manifested in their interpretations of selected texts. Wulf's approach is different from the approaches by Leota and Smith: Firstly, Wulf's approach is ecological. Secondly, as mentioned above, Leota and Smith emphasize the intercultural approach but they do not take colonization and oppression as key to exploring the text. Wulf's approach "does not attempt to revolt against colonizing or oppressive tendencies in [his] specific context as Samoan."[8] However, the postcolonial emphasising of the location or context of a reader is important in his study. Wulf tones down the presence of oppression in his context and in the biblical text, and his challenging of it. An example of this is in Wulf's interpretation of God's "freeing Earth from the bondage of darkness that imprisoned her in the pre-created condition."[9] Wulf does not label his approach as postcolonial, but there are some postcolonial elements in it.

---

[8] Wulf, "Was Earth Created Good?," 37.

[9] Ibid., 184.

Martin Mariota, in his reading of Exod 2–3, appeals to the postcolonial concept of hybridity to define his position as a Samoan reader. Mariota considers himself as a Samoan *Palagi* (European), a hybrid location as a reader. Unlike Leota and Smith, this perspective of hybridity is utilized as a hermeneutic to read the character of Moses in Exod 2–3. For Mariota, that hybrid location is a unique position that gives him access to unique kinds of knowledge. Thus, for Mariota, being in a hybrid location as an Aotearoa New Zealand-born Samoan is "not a position of marginalization or confusion, but instead a place of empowerment."[10] Mariota emphasises the positivity of being a Samoan in a hybrid location at a context outside of Samoa.

In identifying my location as a reader in the Samoan context in relation to the studies by the Samoan scholars discussed above, the drive of my study is different from the studies by Leota and Smith but closer to the studies by Ma'ilo, Wulf, and Mariota. Leota and Smith emphasise only Samoan social and cultural values. Ma'ilo, Wulf, and Mariota consider the colonial and oppressive situations in their contexts which I also emphasise in my location as a reader. The use of my experience and understanding of the Samoan world as a location in third space (hybridity) has closer affinity with Mariota's approach. Like Mariota, I also use the postcolonial notion of hybridity to identify my location in third space as a Samoan reader of the Bible mainly in Samoa. Mariota on the other hand comes to his reading from his situation as an Aotearoa New Zealand-born Samoan.[11]

There are differences between our approaches that I briefly note. First, Mariota defines his hybrid situation as Samoan from the experience of a Samoan born in Aotearoa New Zealand. Because I was born and raised in Samoa, I focus on how the cultures and traditions that have been running and controlling Samoan society are connected to domestic and community problems such as poverty and violence. I am more concerned with how the Christian tradition of discipleship in conjunction with the *matai* hierarchical social and cultural systems overlook the needs and rights of local people.

Second, we label our hybrid situations differently. Mariota labels his hybrid position as "Samoan *Palagi*" while I label my position as *tautuaileva* (service in-between spaces). I see Samoan *Palagi* as a hybrid that highlights the gap between Samoan and *Palagi*, according to which Samoan is one and *Palagi* is the other. Thus, Samoan *Palagi* can be mistaken for two different identities. My hybrid location, on the other hand, has no gaps because *tautuaileva* is at in-between spaces. In fact, in times of undertaking my service role to my family and church, I (re)negotiate the fulfillment of my needs and roles in relation to

---

[10] Mariota, "A Samoan *Palagi*," ix.
[11] Ibid., 1–4.

both. Part of this (re)negotiation involves choosing how to act or respond to needs, according to cultures and values.

In practice, *tautua* (service) uses any culture or material that improves service to the family and community. *Tautua* is not monocultural. It crosses and borrows from other cultures that would serve the needs in the local society. *Tautua* fluctuates, moving in-between places, hence I call my hybrid position *tautuaileva*. It is where I as *tautua* go beyond the familiar spaces of family and village, to enter unfamiliar spaces. Thus, *tautuaileva* as my location in third space is not marginalization but an opportunity to seek other ways to fulfill the needs of the households (family, church, village) to which I belong. It is in this way that *tautuaileva*, as my hybrid position, is the hermeneutic that inform the selection and analysis of the texts.

Tautuaileva Lenses: *Fa'asinomaga, Tautuatoa*

My location in the third space of *tautuaileva* is not static. Rather, it is dynamic and responsive to changes and challenges. It is open to changes from time to time, and from place to place, according to changes and events in those particular places. In the process, *tautuaileva* exposes the marginalized in my world and in the text. It shows that anyone is a *tautua* regardless of gender, status, color, and race. Accordingly, the following categories of my location in third space, *tautuaileva* (service in-between spaces), are the lenses through which I will interpret a selection of texts from Matthew: *fa'asinomaga* (sense of belonging to a place) and *tautuatoa* (courageous serving/servant at a *va*-placement).

Fa'asinomaga

Fa'asinomaga (sense of belonging to a place) is a way of identifying a *tautua* in and through his or her links to a family and village. *Fa'asinomaga* is open to changes and challenges, so my identity is sometimes defined beyond the social and cultural restrictions of family and church. In this way, the *fa'asinomaga* of a *tautua* can extend to other places forming new *fa'asinomaga* of belonging to another place. A *tautua* adapts his or her being Samoan to a new land, home, people, culture, language and relationships, making that new place his or her own. This enables the *tautua* to see the world in the diversity of cultures that run the locality of the world s/he inhabits. This makes the undertaking of *tautua* extend beyond the boundaries of the (original, first, nuclear) family and community.

Another aspect of *fa'asinomaga faatautua* (*tautua*'s sense of belonging) is the relationships (*va fealoa'i*) s/he has with people as well as with social, cultural and religious systems in the (new, hybrid) place that s/he inhabits. There are three functions of *va fealoa'i* in third space: First, *va fealoa'i* designates relationships between people. Second, *va fealoa'i* expresses people's relationships to systems that run and control the local place (e.g., church, village, nation). Third, *va fealoa'i* is not a response in silence to another person, people or system (culture) but making one's voice heard in words and through actions. This requires courage (*toa*, see below). Identifying and defining *va fealoa'i* is in accordance with the *fa'asinomaga* of those in need, and those who help fulfill those needs. More importantly, the *tautua's* sense of belonging to place enables him or her to identify the matters that marginalize her/himself as *tautua*. This is most demanding when the *tautua* is located at in-between-places—the location of *tautuaileva*.

Tautuatoa

Toa means bravery or courage. Added to *tautua* makes *tautuatoa*, which refers to a *tautua* who goes beyond familiar spaces to seek in other spaces ways to improve his or her role as *tautua*. The pathway of *tautuatoa* is action-in-progress. This is where a *tautua* is prepared to face challenges and changes. It makes a *tautua* a courageous and effective *tautai* (fisherperson) and *tufuga* (builder, tattooist). As a *tautai*, s/he is a fisherperson who will go beyond the rough weather in search of fish for the family. As a *tufuga*, s/he will search for the best wood to build a strong house for the family no matter how high the mountains are. *Tautuatoa* has the courage to face any challenge, to break away from familiar norms and traditions, and to enter new spaces where he or she finds ways to fulfill his or her role as a person that belongs to a particular place.

Inthe lights of *fa'asinomaga*, *tautuatoa* involves treating of others with *fa'aaloalo* (respect) and *loto fuatiaifo* (subjectivity). *Tautuatoa* undertaken in-between spaces and relationships enables consideration of the needs of those who are often neglected.

Appropriation

Fa'asinomaga focuses on how a person is linked to a place in regard to land, family (home, house, household), community and titles. Through the *fa'asinomaga* lens I will ask the following questions: How do features of a text, as a narrative and rhetorical unit, reveal the world encoded in the text as a local place? How are characters in the texts linked to land, families, residential places, titles and communities? How do those links develop new or alternative senses of belonging to a local place? How does a new or alternative sense of belonging to place express consideration of the needs of the people in local spaces and societies? Are there good and bad potentials arising from belonging to a place?

Fa'asinomaga is also about different relationships of which local people are a part. These relationships may be old or new. More importantly, the relationships determine how a local person acts the way he or she does. Through the *fa'asinomaga* lens I also ask the following questions of the text: What are the relationships in the texts? Who are in these relationships? How are those relationships linked to the local place? What new relationships are created in the texts? How do people in the texts relate to the social, cultural, economic, political and religious systems in the texts? How do those relationships reflect the needs of people in the texts?

Tautuatoa is about when a *tautua* leaves familiar spaces, such as family or household, and seeks in other spaces alternative ways to fulfill his or her roles as a *tautua*. Breaking away from familiar spaces is in order to (in the end) return to his or her family with new ways to accomplish her/his responsibilities as *tautua*. Thus, through the lens of *tautuatoa*, I will ask the following questions: How do the actions of the people in the texts show service from and in between spaces? What are the familiar spaces from which the characters in the texts break? What new spaces do they enter? How are they described and shown moving to and from spaces? Who in the texts benefits from service from and in between spaces? How does service from and in between spaces reflect Jesus's ministry as place-based discipleship that gives primary attention to the needs, rights, and roles of local people?

Tautuaileva Approach

My *tautuaileva* (service in-between spaces) readings of Matt 4:12–25 and Matt 7:24–8:22 are unavoidably postcolonial. Like Dube's and Wainwright's studies discussed above, my reading identifies my location in Samoan societies appealing to the postcolonial concept of hybridity.[12] Two worlds meet in this study: the world of the text, and my Samoan world. There is a third world as well: the academic world, in and beyond Samoa, into which my reading will be presented and engaged in critical conversation. There is a need to bring these worlds into some form of relationship (*va*, engagement), so that discipleship is explored in conjunction with and acrossmultiple worlds. Gadamer's aesthetic theory provides a backdrop of how I approach the text from multiple worlds.

Gadamer compares the question of meaning to the experience of art. The main question for Gadamer is how can we find the meaning of art or the true beauty of art? Gadamer contends that artwork has the artist's world behind it, for the artist produced the artwork. The art is left by itself and it has its own world. When it is experienced aesthetically by a viewer, it is viewed from the world of the spectator. This experiencing of art is called "play."[13] The spectator has brought to the artwork his or her pre-understanding of the art. At the meeting

---

[12] One important part of this location is my consideration of the women as *tautua* (servant) like men from my point of view as a brother in the sister-brother relationship in *fa'asamoa*.

[13] Hans-Georg Gadamer, *Truth and Method*, trans. Joel Weinsheimer and Donald G. Marshall (New York: Seabury Press, 1975), 91–102.

point, the art is transformed into reality at the moment of viewing. Gadamer talks about "play" as a contemporary movement that brings out the meaning of the art.[14] In connection with the literary text, Gadamer suggests that like the experience of works of art, reading takes place at the moment when the "play movement" occurs. Thus, the task of the reader is to break from the influence of classical hermeneutics which restricts interpretation to one direction.[15] Encountering a work of art or a text, we experience it in relation to our situation and location.

Relating Gadamer's theory to my situation, I already have pre-understanding of discipleship in Matthew's perspective, and that is the traditional understanding of discipleship. Growing up in a Samoan church and community that considers church needs more important than family needs, duties and survival, I accepted that tradition. However, witnessing the impact of that understanding of discipleship on local Samoan families, I began to question passages in Matthew's perspective that show discipleship as a mission where a disciple abandons family to follow Jesus. I thus read for the moment of "play" at which new meanings emerge—inclusive meanings that are appropriate to my concerns. But how can the moment of play produce meanings? Gadamer's "fusion of two horizons" provides a resolution.

Gadamer's "play movement" is an important part of his theory of the "fusion of two horizons."[16] The "play" occurs in the dialogue between the text and the reader. Dialogue forms an understanding of the text and that understanding is the converging of the interpreter's horizon and the horizon of the text.[17] Gadamer suggests that at a certain point, understanding brings about fusion between the text's horizon and the reader's horizon.

In my *tautuaileva* reading, there will be "play" between textual and traditional understandings of discipleship, and between those with the horizons of *fa'aSamoa* (Samoan way) and with the inclusive nature of Jesus's proclamation of ἡ βασιλεία τῶν οὐρανῶν. Part of this "play" is my fluctuating experience in between the margin and centre of Samoan societies, where I realize the contradiction between inequality in traditional discipleship in Samoa, egalitarianism in the *tautua* culture of *fa'aSamoa* and in Jesus's proclamation of God's kingdom. How this experience is utilized in the reading is best described by the postcolonial concept of hybridity, which is the *ileva* part of *tautuaileva*.

---

[14] Ibid., 112–16.

[15] Ibid., 147.

[16] Ibid., 273–81. See also Anthony S. Thiselton, *The Two Horizons: New Testament Hermeneutical Philosophical Description with special reference to Heidegger, Bultmann, Gadamer, and Wittgenstein* (Exeter: Partenoster, 1980), 307–10.

[17] Gadamer, *Truth and Method*, 273.

I will thus explore whether and how the Matthean narrator tells Jesus's ministry (in Matt 4:12–25 and Matt 7:24–8:22) as a mission that gives primary attention to the needs and rights of local people in the local world. I will do this with a reading that fuses *tautuaileva* with sociorhetorical criticism. This fusion allows me to interact with the textualized characters and events, and with the social, cultural, political, and religious systems in the world of the text.[18]

I seek to bring the Matthean perspective into dialogue with the struggles of Samoan *tautua,* for whom the needs of local people are recognized and prioritized. I will do this in and through my exploring the language, narration and progression of the selected texts, analysing how the characters as local people relate to each other, and how and why they act and respond positively to Jesus's ministry. That positive response will be examined for the way it reveals the characters' entering the space of Jesus's ἡ βασιλεία τῶν οὐρανῶν, which is beyond their familiar space, in their search for ways to fulfill their needs and roles as members of local families and households.

I locate myself as a member of the Samoan crowd that seeks ways to improve the situations of local families. Like Wainwright's interpretation, I treat the crowd as a collective character group within the text, comprised of everyone who follows Jesus and who has a chance of becoming a disciple of Jesus. The crowd represents the inclusion of the colonized and marginalized in the world encoded in the text, and as participants in the first century Mediterranean world where Christians' lives were a blending of their environments and the contexts they lived in, with Jesus's vision of ἡ βασιλεία τῶν οὐρανῶν. My *tautuaileva* interpretation will also take into consideration the function of women in the local settings of the first century Mediterranean world.

Conclusion

Tautuaileva foregrounds the needs and rights of local people in the Matthean perspective as well as in Samoan circles. As a social and cultural operation, *tautuaileva* is a caution to those who are leaders not to oppress the people they lead but to serve and to care for their needs.[19] *Tautuaileva* is not about creating revolutionary resistance against community leaders. Rather, it is the beginning for those in need to realize ways that could help move them away from the margin. One such way is to take advantage of available understandings, resources and opportunities in the local worlds. It is about seeking survival in accordance with the reality of life that a person in need encounters.

---

[18] I consider this world as an actual-lived-setting because it has its own language and arrangement in terms of its characters and events as encoded in the text.

[19] Leaders who fail to recognize those in need are to be approached in the Samoan way of *amio fa'aaloalo* (respectable behaviour) and *loto maulalo* (humility).

Entering the third space of *tautuaileva* involves weighing up the opportunities available and deciding on the opportunity that best fulfills the needs of a *tautua*, her/his family and community. The motivation of a *tautua* to enter the third space of *tautuaileva* is her/his realization of the need to seek in other spaces ways to fulfill local needs. This type of *tautua* is a place-based mission to be carried out in relation to the changes occurring in a local community.

In *tautuaileva*, therefore, one breaks away from the familiar spaces of family, church and the norms of traditional discipleship. One enters other spaces, the third space of "service at in-between spaces." In this movement to and from familiar and unfamiliar spaces, *tautuaileva* is not a fixed location but one that is open to changes and challenges.[20]

---

[20] I admit that not all Samoan *tautua* will want to enter *tautuaileva*. That is expected and accepted. Moreover, I welcome challenges and changes to the formulation of *tautuaileva* as hermeneutic in this study.

PART 2

TAUTUAILEVA READINGS

4.

TAUTUAILEVA READING OF MATTHEW 4:12–25

In this chapter I use the *tautuaileva* lenses of *fa'asinomaga* (sense of belonging to a place) and *tautuatoa* (courageous service, servant) to analyse Matt 4:12–25, exploring how Jesus's ministry to Galilee[1] (as encoded in the text) gives primary attention to the needs and rights of local people, the Galileans. In the first section I explain how Matt 4:12–25 is a *siomiaga fa'atusiga* (rhetorical and narrative unit)[2]; in the second section I discuss the inner textures of Matt 4:12–25; in the third section I offer an intertextual analysis of how the Matthean recitation of Isa 8:23–9:1 invites a particular interpretation of Jesus's ministry; and in the fourth section I examine the social and cultural textures of Matt 4:12–25, interpreting Jesus's proclamation of ἡ βασιλεία τῶν οὐρανῶν in the context of Galilee.

This *tautuaileva* reading explores the meanings that Jesus's vision of ἡ βασιλεία τῶν οὐρανῶν offer to the poor and marginalized in the first century Mediterranean social and cultural world. Could Jesus's vision be third space where ἡ βασιλεία τῶν οὐρανῶν is proclaimed in accordance with the world of local Galileans?

---

[1] As mentioned in the introduction, the place of Galilee in understanding Jesus's ministry has been presented from historical, archaeological, and sociological perspectives. See Richard A. Horsley, *Sociology and the Jesus Movement* (New York: Crossroad, 1989); Horsley, *Galilee: History, Politics, People* (Valley Forge: Trinity Press International, 1995); Horsley, *Archaeology, History and Society in Galilee: The Social Context of Jesus and the Rabbis* (Harrisburg: Trinity Press International, 1996); Horsley, "Synagogues in Galilee and the Gospels," in *Evolution of the Synagogue: Problems and Progress*, ed. Howard Clark Kee and Lynn H. Cohick (Harrisburg: Trinity Press International, 1999), 46–69; Richard A. Horsley and John S. Hanson, *Bandits, Prophets, and Messiahs: Popular Movements in the Time of Jesus* (Minneapolis: Winston, 1985); Freyne, *Galilee, Jesus and the Gospels*; Freyne, *Jesus a Jewish Galilean*; Moxnes, "The Construction of Galilee as a Place—Part I," 26–37; Moxnes, "The Construction of Galilee as a Place—Part II," 64–77; Moxnes, *Putting Jesus in Place;* Halvor Moxnes, "Landscape and Spatiality: Placing Jesus," in *Understanding the Social World of the New Testament*, ed. Dietmar Neufeld and Richard E. DeMaris (New York: Routledge, 2010). My focus is on Galilee as a local world.

[2] A rhetorical unit has "a beginning, a middle, and an end" (George Kennedy, *New Testament Interpretation through Rhetorical Criticism* [Chapel Hill: University of North Carolina Press, 1984], 33–34). In the rhetorical unit Matt 4:12–25, Jesus is the main character.

Matt 4:12–25 as Rhetorical and Narrative Unit (*siomiaga fa'atusiga*)

Several scholars (e.g., Kingsbury and Carter[3]) regard the Matthean presentation of Jesus's ministry to begin in Matt 4:17. This claim makes sense because of the phrase, "From that time Jesus began...." There however are two weaknesses in this view in terms of the *tautuaileva* hermeneutic, which considers the sense of belonging of a person to a particular place important. First, this view gives the impression that Jesus's proclamation of ἡ βασιλεία τῶν οὐρανῶν in verse 17 is a separate event from Jesus's dwelling in Capernaum. Second, it isolates Jesus's proclamation of ἡ βασιλεία τῶν οὐρανῶν from Matthew's recitation of Isa 8:23–9:1 which is important in the Matthean announcement of hope for salvation made toward the people of Galilee. From the lens of *fa'asinomaga* which signifies a person in terms of his or her belonging to a place, I take Matt 4:17 as an important part of Jesus's ministry which began with Jesus making his home in Galilee in Matt 4:12. I am thus in agreement with Luz,[4] who also takes the account to begin with Matt 4:12.

In the study of Matthean discipleship, Matt 4:18–22 is usually read as presenting a pattern for discipleship. Matthew 4:18–22 narrates Jesus's calling of the disciples, suggesting that there is a difference between disciples and non-disciples.[5] The calling of the fishermen lays out the pattern for Jesus's calling of his disciples: "Jesus sees, Jesus summons, and at once those summoned leave everything behind."[6] Kingsbury speaks of this pattern as an expression of Jesus's authority to choose who will be his disciples. For Kingsbury, these chosen disciples form a new community which Jesus refers to as his church (Matt 16:18; 18:17) and their goal was to be fishers of men: the mission that the disciples undertake was firstly for Israel and then for the nations (Matt 28:19).

Both Carter and Kingsbury read Matt 4:18–22 as the calling of the first disciples.[7] They exemplify the type of discipleship that follows the traditional

---

[3] See Kingsbury, *Matthew as Story*, 40; Warren Carter, "Kernels and Narrative Blocks: The Structure of Matthew's Gospel," *CBQ* 54.3 (1992): 463–81. For various and different structures of the Gospel of Matthew see David R. Bauer, *The Structure of Matthew's Gospel: A Study in Literary Design* (Sheffield: Sheffield Academic, 1988), 21–56, and M. Eugene Boring, "The Convergence of Source Analysis, Social History, and Literary Structure in the Gospel of Matthew," in *Seminar Papers: Society of Biblical Literature Annual Meeting* (Georgia: Scholars Press, 1994), 587–611.

[4] Luz, *Matthew 1–7*, 194.

[5] Warren Carter, *Matthew: Storyteller, Interpreter, Evangelist* (Peabody: Hendrickson, 1996), 244; Carter, "Matthew 4:18–22," 58–75.

[6] Kingsbury, *Matthew as Story*, 130–31.

[7] Other examples are: Jack D. Kingsbury, "The Verb *AKOLOUTHEIN* ("To Follow") as an Index of Matthew's View of His Community," *JBL* 97 (1978): 56–73; Barton, *Discipleship and Family Ties*, 128–40; Luz, *Matthew 1–7*, 200–201; Carter, "Matthew 4:18–

master-disciple (Jesus-followers) relationship. Such a follower makes a commitment regardless of the life situation he or she encounters. One example of this kind of commitment is the willingness of a follower/disciple to abandon one's family in order to follow Jesus, the master. In the eyes of *tautuaileva*, in which the connection of a follower to a local place is significant, this kind of understanding has a one-dimensional focus on discipleship that overlooks the connections of people to local families and households, and Jesus's relationship to the crowd in the local place of Galilee. For example, the families that the fishermen left behind are drawn into the interpretation of this passage from the point of view of ecclesiological and global mission. If discipleship is based only on Jesus's direct calling of a person to follow him, the function of Jesus's authority revealed in his actions, such as the healing of people, is overlooked as another way of Jesus's calling a disciple.

Both Jesus's words and his actions in the activities of his ministry are important. I look at the Matthean presentation of the beginning of Jesus's ministry in Matt 4:12–16, where Jesus withdraws from Judea and makes his home in Capernaum, Galilee. This is followed by Jesus's first announcement of ἡ βασιλεία τῶν οὐρανῶν in Matt 4:17. In the progression of events as Jesus's ministry develops in the Matthean account, the calling of the fishermen to follow in Matt 4:18–22 is the first result of Jesus's dwelling in Capernaum. Jesus's calling of the four brothers to follow him links to Jesus's making his home in Capernaum in Matt 4:12–16, and Jesus's going throughout Galilee in 4:23–25 which culminates in the following of the great crowd in Matt 4:25. In this way, calling someone to follow includes both the consequences of Jesus's words and his actions *in a particular place*, such as his teachings, preaching, and healings in Galilee. Anyone who responds positively to Jesus's teachings, preaching and healings, are Jesus's disciples also. This chapter will explore, with the sentiments of *tautuaileva*, how Matt 4:12–25 as a rhetorical and narrative unit contains local place-based discipleship that allows for many (who were not called) to be disciples of Jesus.

Jesus and the Crowd are Local Galileans

One of the concerns of *fa'asinomaga* is how a text tells and shows the world encoded in the text as a local place, and how the text presents the local people of that place. In this subsection, the opening and closing signs of Matt 4:12–25 are

---

22 and the Matthean Discipleship," 58–75; Howell, *Matthew's Inclusive Story: A Study in the Narrative Rhetoric*, 53.

interpreted as an *inclusio* that indicate Galilee as the local place, and the characters of Jesus and the crowd are people belonging to that place.[8]

The opening signs of the rhetorical unit are in verse 12: Ἀκούσας δὲ ὅτι Ἰωάννης παρεδόθη ἀνεχώρησεν εἰς τὴν Γαλιλαίαν (But when Jesus heard that John had been arrested, he withdrew to Galilee). First, the δὲ (but) conjunction indicates a shift from the previous events (Jesus's baptism and temptation) to the next (Jesus's withdrawal to Galilee). The shift anticipates the beginning of a new event which is Jesus's dwelling in Galilee and his proclamation of ἡ βασιλεία τῶν οὐρανῶν there. Second, the connection of verse 12 to the previous activities presents Jesus as the protagonist. Third, verse 12 positions Galilee as the rhetorical space where the audience of the first activities of Jesus's ministry are found.

The closing indicators of the unit are in verse 25: καὶ ἠκολούθησαν αὐτῷ ὄχλοι πολλοὶ ἀπὸ τῆς Γαλιλαίας (And great crowds followed him from Galilee). First, καὶ (and) indicates that the unit is coming to a conclusion. Second, the following of the great crowds is the result of Jesus's withdrawal to Galilee. Third, Galilee as the place where the great crowds come in conjunction with the mention of Galilee in the opening of the unit (v. 12) forms the rhetorical frame that surrounds the beginning activities of Jesus's ministry in the Matthean text. In other words, Galilee is the local place encoded in this unit.

The following analysis is based on the threefold structure of the rhetorical unit that reveals the significance of Galilee as a local place in which Jesus's ministry begins in the Matthean story:

1. Matt 4:12–16 *Amataga* (Beginning): Jesus makes his home in Galilee;
2. Matt 4:17–22 *Ogatotonu* (Middle): Jesus ministers to the first members of the crowd near the Sea of Galilee;
3. Matt 4:23–25 *Fa'aiuga* (End): Jesus ministers to other members of the crowd from Galilee.

The unit begins with the narrator explaining the reason why Jesus withdraws to Galilee. Jesus's name is not mentioned in Matt 4:12–16, but the conjunction δὲ (but) in verse 12 connects the event of dwelling in Galilee to Jesus's temptation (Matt 4:1–11) and the activities of John the Baptist (3:1–17). Δὲ as a conjunction has multiple functions such as transition, continuity, and

---

[8] *Inclusio* is "signs of opening and closure." See Kennedy, *New Testament Interpretation*, 34, 82. See also Charles H. Lohr, "Oral Techniques in Gospel of Matthew," *CBQ* 23.4 (1961): 408–10. Lohr claims that Matthew is very fond of this device.

contrast,[9] and in this part of the unit it links Jesus's move to Galilee with the previous events. As a transition, δὲ marks the shift of the story from John's arrest, indicating the end of John's ministry, to Jesus's dwelling in Galilee. As a marker of contrast, δὲ signals the contrast between John and Jesus as proclaimers of ἡ βασιλεία τῶν οὐρανῶν. As an indicator of continuity, δὲ points to Jesus's dwelling in Capernaum as a continuation of the mission of ἡ βασιλεία τῶν οὐρανῶν that John started. Jesus is the subject of the verb ἀκούσας (he heard) thus moving to Galilee makes Jesus belong to Galilee.

The connection of Matt 4:12–25 to Matt 4:1–11 is important in providing the backdrop for Jesus's withdrawal and his making of his home in Galilee (Matt 4:12–16). This is accentuated by the use of the adverb of time τότε (then) in Matt 3:5, 13; 4:1, 5, 10, 11. This τότε points to ἐν δὲ ταῖς ἡμέραις ἐκείναις (But in those days) in Matt 3:1 which are the days of John the Baptist. What happens in Matt 4:12–25 has literary connections to the events that have gone before. This locates the beginning of Jesus's ministry at Matt 4:12 (when Jesus withdraws to Capernaum), rather than with Matt 4:17 as Kingsbury and Carterproposed.[10] In verse 17, Jesus takes up in Galilee the ministry that John had been doing at the Jordan in Judea; so Jesus extends the location of John's vision and proclamation.

After moving to Galilee (Matt 4:12–16), Jesus made the first public declaration of the aim of his ministry—ἡ βασιλεία τῶν οὐρανῶν[11] (4:17)—and he called the fishermen to follow him (4:18–22). Asa reader who considers the family very important, I am surprised by the response of the fishermen—they left their families and followed Jesus. Considering that, at the narrative level, Jesus has no prior contact with the four fishermen, the four brothers' immediate response to Jesus creates a rhetorical hiatus. Questions arise concerning the function of calling these four fishermen in this part of Jesus's ministry. Traditionally, it has been interpreted to indicate that the first called disciples of Jesus were distinctive from the great crowd mentioned in Matt 4:25.[12]

---

[9] See Stephanie Black, *Sentence Conjunctions in the Gospel of Matthew: καὶ, δὲ, τότε, γάρ, οὖν, and Asyndeton in Narrative Discourse* (Sheffield: Sheffield Academic, 2002), 142–78.

[10] Jack D. Kingsbury, *Matthew: Structure, Christology, Kingdom* (Philadelphia: Fortress, 1975), 7; Carter, "Kernels and Narrative Blocks," 463–81.

[11] These words of Eduard Schweizer nicely sums up Jesus's withdrawal to Galilee as asserted in my interpretation: "Jesus' move to 'Galilee of gentiles' demonstrates God's amazing initiative toward those who had never even been considered." Eduard Schweizer, *The Good News According to Matthew*, trans. David E. Green (London: Westminster John Knox, 1975), 68.

[12] Despite the lack of information about the four brothers, their immediate positive response has been interpreted as reflecting the power and authority of the creative word of God in and through Jesus proclamation of ἡ βασιλεία τῶν οὐρανῶν. Richard A. Edwards

A close analysis of the calling of the four fishermen reveals another role and function. The fishermen's presence in the middle section illustrates the kind of people mentioned in the recitation of the prophecy of Isaiah in Matt 4:15–16: they are Galileans sitting in darkness, who have seen a great light. Thus, the following of the fishermen is an illustration of how members that made up the crowd responded to Jesus's proclamation of ἡ βασιλεία τῶν οὐρανῶν. In other words, the fishermen are examples of people from the local place of Galilee who respond positively to Jesus's proclamation of ἡ βασιλεία τῶν οὐρανῶν.

The lens of *fa'asinomaga* shows the significance of Galilee as a local space, in which Jesus's ministry begins and the place where his first audience, the first members of the crowd, gathered. The arrangement begins with the commonplace and its description (4:12–16). The place is in Galilee, near the sea in the lands of Zebulun and Naphtali. It is also described as a place of gentiles beyond Jordan.[13] Jesus's dwelling in Capernaum suggests that he had a sense of belonging to Galilee. It evokes an expectation that something important will occur in Galilee. It also evokes the question of the motivation for Jesus making his home in Galilee. In the Matthean perspective, it was to fulfill what the prophet Isaiah said:

> Land of Zebulun, land of Naphtali, on the road by the sea, across the Jordan, Galilee of gentiles—the people who sat in darkness have seen a great light, and for those who sat in the region and shadow of death light has dawned. (Matt 4:15–16)

The next part of the unit (Matt 4:17–22) focuses on the first activities of Jesus in Galilee. It begins with the announcement of ἡ βασιλεία τῶν οὐρανῶν (Matt

---

argues that Jesus's command is a reason for their immediate following. Edwards, *Matthew's Narrative Portrait of Disciples*, 19–22. See also John P. Meier, *Matthew* (Dublin: Veritas Publications, 1980), 34.

Reading from the point of view of the members of the crowd who saw and heard Jesus for the first time, the positive response is problematic. I argue below that Matthew's use of Περιπατῶν as a verbal adjective in verse 18 states that Jesus's "walk" by the sea is a form of proclaiming ἡ βασιλεία τῶν οὐρανῶν (mentioned in verse 17). It was not just a walk; it was the proclamation of ἡ βασιλεία τῶν οὐρανῶν. The four brothers responded accordingly, near the sea.

[13] H. Dixon Slingerland claimed that Matt 4:15 is one of the references that show where Matthew's gospel was composed. For Slingerland, it reveals that Matthew's Gospel was composed in the east side of Jordan River not in Syria Antioch as many scholars claimed. H. Dixon Slingerland, "The Trans jordanian Origin of St. Matthew's Gospel," *JSNT* 18.3 (1979): 18–28. I will suggest later that Matthew's recitation of Isa 8:23 (MT) in Matt 4:15 shows the theological significance of "Zebulun and Naphtali, on the road by the sea, across the Jordan," as locations of hope for Jews and gentiles.

4:17), followed by the call of the four fishermen (Matt 4:18–22). Jesus's command demonstrates his authority to bring people into his ministry and to help those in need. Jesus as a Galilean has authority to make fellow Galileans (who sit in darkness and the shadow of death) have a positive sense of their being Galileans. The final part of the unit (Matt 4:23–25) refers to the following of the great crowd as the climax of the first activities of Jesus's ministry in Galilee.

How does the rhetorical arrangement affect the purposes suggested above? The innertexture of the unit reveals the involvement of the crowd. They are the local people of Galilee whose movements suggest they are breaking away from oppressive and colonial spaces, seeking to enter liberating spaces such as Jesus's ἡ βασιλεία τῶν οὐρανῶν.

Inner-textures: *Fa'asinomaga* and *Tautuatoa*

How does Matt 4:12–25 present Galilee as a local place? How does this unit show Jesus's sense of belonging to that local place? How do literary features of this unit portray the crowd and their sense of belonging to Galilee? How does the narrator tell and show Jesus's relationship to members of the crowd? How is that relationship linked to the local place?

Through the lenses of *fa'asinomaga* and *tautuatoa*, this analysis explores how the language, narration, and progression of Matt 4:12–25 reveal the crowd's sense of belonging within Galilee, and how Jesus's relationship to the crowd demonstrates the challenges they must overcome in order to fulfill their needs and strengthen their sense of belonging to Galilee.

Matt 4:12–16

There are many interpretations of why Jesus withdraws to Capernaum. One interpretation is that this was Jesus's reaction to John's arrest. He moved to Capernaum as a way of offering resistance against the Roman imperial power.[14] Another interpretation is that Jesus's withdrawal to Galilee is to show that the "rejection of God's word in one place leads to the proclamation of it to another."[15] These interpretations show that Jesus's return to Galilee is prompted by John's arrest.

In my *tautuaileva* eyes, it is significant that Galileans (gentiles) will be the first recipients of Jesus's proclamation of ἡ βασιλεία τῶν οὐρανῶν. The undertaking of discipleship as a local place-based ministry began in Galilee. Jesus's

---

[14] Warren Carter, "Evoking Isaiah: Matthean Soteriology and An Intertextual Reading of Isaiah 7–9 and Matthew 1:23 and 4:15–16," *JBL* 119 (2000): 503–20; Fernando Bermejo-Rubio, "(Why) Was Jesus the Galilean Crucified Alone? Solving a False Conundrum," *JSNT* 36.2 (2013): 127–54.

[15] David Hill, *The Gospel of Matthew*, NCB (London: Butler & Tanner, 1972), 103.

withdrawal to Capernaum is prompted not just by John's arrest but by the will of God as revealed in Isaiah's prophecy recited in Matt 4:14–15. Jesus's withdrawal to Capernaum is not in defeat, but in order to fulfil scripture.

Through the lens of *fa'asinomaga*, the words ἀκούσας δὲ ὅτι Ἰωάννης παρεδόθη (But when Jesus heard that John had been arrested) (v. 12) is the time of withdrawal to Galilee to begin his ministry. The exact time or day that John was arrested is not mentioned.[16] John's arrest indicates that his involvement in this part of the story comes to an end. It is now Jesus's turn. The words ἐν δὲ ταῖς ἡμέραις ἐκείναις (But in those days) in Matt 3:1 speak of the time when Jesus was living in Nazareth (Matt 2:23). In those days John the Baptist proclaimed ἡ βασιλεία τῶν οὐρανῶν in the wilderness of Judea and baptised people in the river Jordan, Jesus being one of them (Matt 3:1–17). After baptism, Jesus returned to Capernaum instead of Nazareth,[17] where his family lived. Capernaum was anticipated by Isaiah, because it was near the sea.[18]

In entering Capernaum, Jesus entered a borderland space; a space, away from his family, from where he could reach out to the people of Galilee in accordance with his vision of ἡ βασιλεία τῶν οὐρανῶν. The description of the territory in Matt 4:15–16 depicts a borderland space inhabited by different kinds of people. That space according to the Matthean narrator is a land on the road, by the sea, across the Jordan. It is that space in which Jesus located himself and from which he will reach out to those who need help. In this way, Galilee functions as the image of ἡ βασιλεία τῶν οὐρανῶν for those who embrace Jesus's ministry. Jesus dwelling there transforms the borderland into a great place to live in.

In her study of the kingdom of heaven in Matthew, Margaret Pamment claims that ἡ βασιλεία τῶν οὐρανῶν "refers to a wholly future reality which is imminent." This is reflected in the meaning of ἤγγικεν as "has drawn near and not yet arrived."[19] Alternatively, Margaret Hannan argues that Matthew's utili-

---

[16] Historically, the time of John's arrest was when Herod Antipas ruled Galilee on behalf of the Roman emperor. See Sean Freyne, "Herodian Economics in Galilee: Searching for a Suitable Model," in *Modelling early Christianity: Social-Scientific Studies of the New Testament in Its Context*, ed. Philip F. Esler (New York: Routledge, 1995), 23–46; Peter Richardson, *Herod: King of the Jews and Friend of the Romans* (Columbia: University of South Carolina Press, 1996).

[17] Why Jesus left Nazareth and chose Capernaum as residence is of no interest to Luz (*Matthew 1–7*, 194).

[18] See Donald A. Hagner, *Matthew 1–13*, WBC 33a (Nashville: Thomas Nelson, 2000), 72; W. D. Davies and Dale C. Allison, *A Critical and Exegetical Commentary on the Gospel according to Saint Matthew I–VII*, ICC (Edinburgh: T&T Clark, 1988), 376–78; Craig A. Evans, NCBC (Cambridge: Cambridge University Press, 2012), 88–89.

[19] Margaret Pamment, "The Kingdom of Heaven According to the First Gospel," *NTS* 27.2 (1981): 211–32. For a reading that is critical of Pamment's interpretation see Robert

zation of the perfect tense in Matt 4:17 indicates that the kingdom of heavens as an event that has already happened in the past and is continuing to the present.[20] Matthew's use of the second aorist in describing the coming Kingdom of the Father (Matt 10:23, 13:41, 16:27–28) points to an event that has not yet ended. For Hannan, these different tenses suggest that ἡ βασιλεία τῶν οὐρανῶν deals with the reality of life on earth, reflecting the continuation to the present of the activities of the sovereign God.

I agree with Hannan. There are temporal and spatial significances of ἡ βασιλεία τῶν οὐρανῶν. It is about the reality of the world, so it could be regarded as referring to a local βασιλεία and this is reflected in Moxnes' interpretation in relation to issues with local families and households in which the kingdom of God is heralded as an "imagined place."[21] The kingdom of God, as such, is a third space. Thus, ἡ βασιλεία τῶν οὐρανῶν "present(s) visions or plans for alternative ways to use and structure places and material practices."[22]

In considering ἡ βασιλεία τῶν οὐρανῶν as a third space, Capernaum is seen as an "imagined space" that exhibits a vision of how the local people of Galilee on the margin may face the realities of the world. The local people of Capernaum are to live ἡ βασιλεία τῶν οὐρανῶν in accordance with the reality of life in Galilee. As such, ἡ βασιλεία τῶν οὐρανῶν is a borderland that a local Galilean chose as the space that will help him or her fulfill roles and responsibilities to a local family or household. In this way, Jesus's return to Capernaum Galilee fulfills the prophecy of Isaiah regarding God's promise of hope and restoration for the displaced people in Galilee—both Jews and gentiles.

Jesus's move to Galilee was in the interest of the people in Galilee. This is the view also held by Deidre Good, who interprets Jesus's move to Galilee as part of the motif of withdrawal in Matthew's account. This motif has a threefold pattern: "hostility/withdrawal/prophetic." [23] The "function of this pattern throughout the gospel is to move the narrative along."[24] Warren Carter adds another dimension. For Carter, Jesus dwells in Galilee not to hide himself from the Romans but to begin there the works of God's rule in and through his actions, the resistance to the Roman Empire.[25] Thus, the first recipients of God's salvation are the people oppressed and colonized by the Roman imperial power.

Foster, "Why on Earth Use 'Kingdom of Heaven'? Matthew's Terminology Revisited," *NTS* 48.4 (2002): 487–99.

[20] Margaret Hannan, *The Nature and Demands of the Sovereign Rule of God in the Gospel of Matthew* (New York: T&T Clark International, 2006), 34, 230–32.

[21] Moxnes, *Putting Jesus in His Place*, 108–09.

[22] Ibid., 109.

[23] Deidre Good, "The Verb ΑΝΑΧΩΡΕΩ in Matthew's Gospel," *NovT* 32 (1990): 2–3.

[24] Ibid., 1.

[25] See Carter, "Evoking Isaiah," 503–20. According to Meier, "Jesus can hardly be seeking refuge as he marches into Galilee, the territory of Herod Antipas, who has just

In the *tautuatoa* lens, Jesus withdraws as a courageous servant. He entered a borderland space in order to reach out to the local people, to help them gain a sense of belonging. Jesus presented them with a "borderland space" in his vision of ἡ βασιλεία τῶν οὐρανῶν. As such, Jesus as *tautuatoa* seeks to make the people of Capernaum feel more comfortable and confident living in Galilee.

Jesus's move to Galilee fulfills Isaiah's prophecy, as could be seen in the chiasmus[26] in Matt 4:13–15.

{Jesus withdrew to Galilee (v. 12)}
    A. Beside the sea in the territory of Zebulun and Naphtali (v. 13)
        B. What had been spoken through Isaiah might be fulfilled (v. 14)
    A'. Land of Zebulun, land of Naphthali, by the sea...Galilee (v. 15)
{The people who sat in darkness have seen a great light, and for those who sat in the region and shadow of death (v. 16)}

Verses 12 and 16 frame the chiasmus. This frame highlights Galilee and its people, who once sat in darkness and the shadow of death but now light has dawned upon them. Zebulun and Naphtali near the Sea of Galilee are explicitly mentioned as the place in Galilee to which Jesus has moved. The centre of the chiasmus speaks of Jesus's dwelling in Galilee as the fulfillment of Isaiah's prophecy. Thus, Galilee the place where Jesus's ministry begins is "the place of light"[27] and it is an important place in this part of the narrative. With the lens of *fa'asinomaga*, Jesus would have gained a sense of belonging to Galilee.

---

imprisoned John." Meier adds, "Jesus is consciously taking up John's fallen banner and continuing in the teeth of opposition" (Meier, *Matthew*, 32). Fernando Bermejo-Rubio asserts that Jesus's ministry was of resistance against the Roman power. "The widespread notion that Jesus could not be involved in significant anti-Roman activity because his followers were not crucified with him is nothing more than paralogism" (Bermejo-Rubio, "Why Was Jesus the Galilean Crucified Alone?," 127–54). Jesus in this way is a good example of a *tautuatoa*. Everything that is happening in this part of the story is for the local people in the local place of Galilee.

[26] See James L. Bailey and Lyle D. Vander Broek, *Literary Forms in the New Testament: A Handbook* (Louisville: Westminster John Knox, 1992), 178–83; Kennedy, *New Testament Interpretation*, 11–12, 28–29, 61.

[27] According to France, Matthew's use of Isa 9:1–2 indicates "Galilee as the place of light" (R. T. France, *The Gospel of Matthew*, NICNT [Grand Rapids: Eerdmans, 2007], 139). I agree that Matthew's recitation of Isa 8:23–9:1 announces the arrival of hope for the people in Galilee whom, according to the context of Isaiah, God punished for their disobedience.

Matt 4:17–22

Through the lens of *tautuatoa*, the innertexture of the middle part of the unit reveals two things: first, it reveals the message of Jesus's ministry and its beginning as a challenge to the local people of Galilee; second, it reveals the first courageous members of the crowd as fishermen. A fisherman in Samoa is *tautai* (master fisherperson), who is a courageous *tautua* who brings fish for the family despite rough weather and seas. It is also used as a metaphorical name for a *tautua* who, despite the difficulties, presses forward looking for opportunities to improve her/his role as *tautua*. S/he enters unfamiliar spaces where opportunities are. Such a *tautai* is a *tautuatoa*.

Jesus is the first example of *tautuatoa* in this middle part of the unit, through his words and actions.[28] Musa Dube's explanation resonates with my *tautuaileva* reading:

> our Christian traditions often name Jesus for us. But which traditions—
> oppressive or liberating ones? Jesus asks us *'Who do you say that I am?'* and so
> it is insufficient for us to retain and use only the received Christology. Rather,
> we must name Christ for ourselves.[29]

On Dube's invitation, I choose to look at Jesus as a courageous servant, thus echoing Lidjia Novakovic's consideration of "Servant of God:"[30]

---

[28] Identifying who Jesus is in Matthew is a huge task beyond the scope of this study. See Dennis C. Duling, "The Therapeutic Son of David: An Element in Matthew's Christological Apologetic," *NTS* 24.3 (1978): 392–410. Elaine M. Wainwright, *Shall We Look for Another? A Feminist Rereading of the Matthean Jesus* (Maryknoll: Orbis, 1998); Wainwright, "Reading Matthew 3–4," 25–43; Kingsbury, *Matthew as Story*, 43–58; Ulrich Luz, "The Son of Man in Matthew: Heavenly Judge or Human Christ," *JSNT* 48 (1992): 3–21; Walter T. Wilson, "The Uninvited Healer: Houses, Healing and Prophets in Matthew 8:1–22," *JSNT* 36 (2013): 53–72; Bruce J. Malina and Jerome H. Neyrey, *Calling Jesus Names: The Social Value of Labels in Matthew* (Sonoma: Polebridge Press, 1988). Richard Bauckham, "The Son of Man: a 'Man in My Position' or 'Someone'?," *JSNT* 23 (1985): 23–33.

[29] Musa W. Dube, "Who Do You Say that I am?" *FTh* 15.3 (2007): 346–67.

[30] See debate on Jesus as Son of God and Servant of God by Jack D. Kingsbury, "The Figure of Jesus in Matthew's Story: A Literary-Critical Probe," *JSNT* 21 (1984): 3–36; "The Figure of Jesus in Matthew's Story A Rejoinder to David Hill," *JSNT* 25 (1985): 61–81, and David Hill, "Son and Servant: an Essay on Matthean Christology," *JSNT* 6 (1980): 2–16. Kingsbury argues that Matthew's Jesus should be understood as Son of God, based on the baptism in 3:16–17. According to Hill, however, Kingsbury's argument is problematic for he ignores the importance of other sources used by Matthew such as the Old Testament citations.

the label "Servant of God," whether in Greek or Hebrew, is never treated as a title like Christ. It does not appear in Jewish literature in statements like "So and so is the servant of the Lord." Even in the NT, the 'Servant of God' is not treated like a title: Jesus is never confessed to be the 'servant'. The reason for this seems to be quite obvious: the term 'servant' could be applied to many different personalities and had no specific content. Broadly speaking, 'God's servant' was an appropriate term for everyone who has been faithful to God.[31]

I take "servant of God" as a *tautua*, which applies to anyone who is faithful to God. The faithfulness of Jesus[32] in proclaiming ἡ βασιλεία τῶν οὐρανῶν in Capernaum, shows him as a servant of God. The following analysis reflects this attribute of Jesus.

In Jesus's first announcement of ἡ βασιλεία τῶν οὐρανῶν (4:17), the narrator's use of ἀπο τότε (from then) signals the time of his proclamation, namely, when Jesus made his home in Capernaum. It foreshadows the proclamation of ἡ βασιλεία τῶν οὐρανῶν. Matthew's use of ἤρξατο (he began; an aorist middle verb) to describe Jesus's beginning of his ministry is important. The aorist middle voice indicates the subject (of the verb) acting upon itself. Jesus is the agent of ἡ βασιλεία τῶν οὐρανῶν on earth; he takes upon himself the responsibility of proclaiming that βασιλεία. This is a characteristic of a *tautuatoa*, especially a *tautai* (fisherperson).

Jesus as the agent of ἡ βασιλεία τῶν οὐρανῶν guarantees that repentance can make a person become a member of the kingdom. But who would accept this kind of proclamation? The local could question who this Jesus was. Jesus was new to Capernaum, so not many would know who he was. Believing in Jesus's ministry and accepting his proclamation in this early stage of his ministry would have been a challenge to local Galileans. Thus, anyone from Capernaum who responded positively to Jesus's ministry must have had courage. In the lens of *fa'asinomaga*, repentance is one significant obligation for belonging to Galilee, the first local place in which God's work of salvation takes place. Repentance involves changing one's mind by moving from one space (unbelieving) to another (believing), and this is another characteristic of a *tautuatoa*.

The imperative μετανοεῖτε that begins the announcement is derived from the verb μετανοέω which means "to change one's mind" or "to be converted."[33]

---

[31] Lidija Novakovic, "Matthew's Atomistic Use of the Scripture: Messianic Interpretation of Isaiah 53:4 in Matthew 8:17," in *Biblical Interpretation in Early Christian Gospels*, ed. Thomas R. Hatina, vol. 2 (London: T&T Clark International, 2008), 154.

[32] Jesus as a healer in Matthew is an important characteristic of Jesus as the Son of God (Duling, "The Therapeutic Son of David," 399). The significance of Jesus as healer, is also reflected in Wainwright's consideration of Jesus as "the holy one of God through whom God, the healer in Israel, heals."

[33] *BDAG*, s.v. "Μετανοέω."

Combined with ἡ βασιλεία τῶν οὐρανῶν the imperative brings out the repentance element in the announcement.[34] This is reflected in Matthew's use of the perfect tense ἤγγικεν (it has come near) to indicate that God's past activities, including God's dealing with Israel. As Hannan reads it, repentance in Matthew "stresses the mutual fidelity of the covenant partners."[35] This shows God's persistent revealing of his sovereignty on behalf of Israel, as a chosen nation that includes anyone who accepts Jesus's ministry by living in accordance with God's will. In this way, repentance as part of this first announcement of ἡ βασιλεία τῶν οὐρανῶν is hope for the local Galileans to restore their relationship with God. This enables them to come out of their oppressive ways of living, and from under the authority of Roman imperial power.

Calling people to repent opens the way to bring the people of Galilee into ἡ βασιλεία τῶν οὐρανῶν. The fishermen's response (4:20, 22) and the bringing of the sick to Jesus (4:24), show that the people of Galilee were beginning to respond to Jesus's ministry. With the lens of *fa'asinomaga*, I see Jesus giving primary attention to the local people in need.

The importance of ἡ βασιλεία τῶν οὐρανῶν is evident in the form of a command, presented as an enthymeme:[36] *Repent, for the kingdom of heaven has come near.* The major premise of this enthymeme is in a construction of a rhetorical syllogism, namely, that ἡ βασιλεία τῶν οὐρανῶν is here. It is on earth for everyone, but what determines its arrival is not known. In order for this enthymeme to make sense, the major premise needs to be ascertained. The minor premise to "repent" is the reason why the announcement of ἡ βασιλεία τῶν οὐρανῶν is made, namely, that there is sin.[37] The announcement is actually the conclusion of an apparent syllogism which is "those who repent will become

---

[34] Hannan, *The Nature and Demands*, 34. This interpretation shows repentance as a relational phenomenon where one repents not just for the sake of his or her own person but for others—his or her family or community.

[35] Ibid.

[36] An enthymeme is a rhetorical syllogism that is assumed from general and special truths (see Aristotle, *Art of Rhetoric*, trans. J. H. Freese [Massachusetts: Harvard, 1991], xxxvi–xxxvii). It is a statement that infers a proposition or shows arriving at a conclusion. See also Burton L. Mack, *Rhetoric and the New Testament* (Minneapolis: Fortress, 1990), 38–39. Kennedy, *New Testament Interpretation*, 16–17.

[37] Repentance emphasised in Matthew is not an individual person's repentance but a repentance of a group of people as a community including its values and systems such as its social, cultural, and political structures. See Davies and Allison, *A Critical and Exegetical Commentary Matthew I–VII*, 306–07. Although Jesus's proclamation of ἡ βασιλεία τῶν οὐρανῶν reflects Israel's ongoing disobedience, its most important function is to reveal the chance for restoration of the covenant between God and the people which is not just for the Jews but for the gentiles as well. See Hannan, *The Nature and Demands*, 34.

members of ἡ βασιλεία τῶν οὐρανῶν." Presenting this first announcement of ἡ βασιλεία τῶν οὐρανῶν as an enthymeme that follows after the narrator's inclusion of Isaiah's prophecy in verses 15–16 is important. It points in an emphatic way to the purpose of Jesus's ministry and how it should be received by those sitting in darkness. With the lens of *fa'asinomaga*, Jesus brings light so that the local Galileans could deal with the reality of life in Galilee. The ministry of Jesus is about ἡ βασιλεία τῶν οὐρανῶν being the space that the local people of Galilee could enter in order to satisfy their needs. Coming out of darkness in order to enter this space of light is a decision and an action of *tautuatoa*.

Verses 18–22 begin to show how Jesus's proclamation of ἡ βασιλεία τῶν οὐρανῶν becomes a great light. Jesus walking near the Sea of Galilee is the action of a *tautuatoa*. This includes, in particular, his activities near the sea before calling the fishermen. The conjunction δὲ (but) in verse 18 indicates that the event in verses 18–22 is part of Jesus's proclamation of ἡ βασιλεία τῶν οὐρανῶν in verse 17. It contrasts between proclaiming ἡ βασιλεία τῶν οὐρανῶν in words (v. 17) and in actions (verses 18–22). The verbal adjective Περιπατων (having walked) in verse 18 suggests that Jesus's walk beside the Sea of Galilee is a proclamation of the kingdom to people beside the sea. The response of the four fishermen is thus not surprising. The fishermen understood Jesus's (walking) ministry and that made them leave their families and follow him. The *tautuaileva* hermeneutic depicts the four fishermen as *tautai* who will seek ways to improve the situations in which their families have been embroiled. This blending of real fishing and metaphoric fishing is one example of how local Galileans could lighten their struggles by following the light of Jesus's proclamation. Such blending is an example of considering Jesus's vision of ἡ βασιλεία τῶν οὐρανῶν as third (in-between).

Matt 4:23–25

Verse 23 begins with the conjunction καὶ (and), linking the end of the unit (verses 23–25) to the previous parts and showing the ongoing development of the crowd (Matt 4:25). After Jesus called the four fishermen he then went throughout Galilee proclaiming ἡ βασιλεία τῶν οὐρανῶν by teaching, preaching, and healing. Matthew's use of περιῆγεν (he was walking) as imperfect tense suggests that these activities were repeated more than once. Jesus exhibits two characteristics of a proclaimer of ἡ βασιλεία τῶν οὐρανῶν.

First, he goes around seeking those who need help. Jesus takes his ministry to another level by going to the people of Galilee and beyond, from a small to a larger space in Galilee, and from a small to a large group of Galilean people. The group of people said to have connected to Jesus's ministry begins with those metaphorically sitting in darkness (4:15–16) and grew to include the great crowd that followed Jesus (4:25). The progression shows that the prophecy in verses 14–15 affirms the different kinds of people that Jesus will deal with in Galilee. The unit then moves to show the kind of response needed (as modelled by the four fishermen). The development continues to show a large group of people in 4:23–25 whom Jesus heals, and to whom he teaches and preaches the vision of ἡ βασιλεία τῶν οὐρανῶν. It culminates with the mention of the great crowd as a designation of the largest group, thereby bringing together all the people in, around, and beyond Galilee. In this way, Galilee is where the people from other cities and places come to seek help in Jesus's ministry. This being the case, the crowd features as a significant character group within this unit. At the beginning of the unit (4:12), Jesus makes his home in Galilee and then the unit moves on to show Jesus walking around Galilee near the sea. Jesus's movement changes from dwelling to walking and then ends with him going throughout Galilee. The development of Jesus's movement in this unit displays the locality of Jesus's ministry.

Second, Jesus is also characterized as a healer. According to Duling, Jesus is the therapeutic Son of David in Matthew, demonstrated by Matthew's preference for the verb θεραπεύω (I heal).[38] Likewise, Wainwright looks at Jesus as "the holy one of God through whom God, the healer in Israel, heals." Like Duling, Wainwright points out that Matthew's use of the verb θεραπεύω indicates the significance of Jesus as healer. Wainwright adds that "in the Matthean context, healing is intimately linked to preaching and teaching and is the work of the holy one of God."[39] I agree with Duling and Wainwright based on the use of θεραπεύω, "to heal or restore." It also means to serve. In fact, the task of healing in this passage (4:12–25) is a service that Jesus does in Galilee.

Jesus is a *tautuatoa*. He goes throughout Galilee more than once. He repeatedly leaves the space he is familiar with to enter new spaces in order to help those in need there. As a recent resident of Capernaum, Jesus performs the works of an uninvited person who has courage to seek and help those in need. Thus, despite Jesus being a new person in Capernaum, how he carries out his ministry makes Capernaum his *fa'asinomaga*. Jesus the Son of God, as declared in Matt 3:16, is a courageous servant—a *tautuatoa*.

---

[38] Duling, "The Therapeutic Son of David," 399.

[39] Wainwright, *Women Healing*, 142.

The Crowd as Tautuatoa

The ὄχλοι is mentioned once in the conclusion of this unit (Matt 4:25).[40] That ὄχλοι is made up of all the people in the progression of this rhetorical unit beginning with verse 12 and ending in verse 25. The unit concludes with καὶ ἠκολούθησαν ὄχλοι πολλοι (And great crowds followed him [Matt 4:25]), which presents (through the combination of the conjunction καὶ (and) with the verb ἠκολούθησαν (they followed) the great crowd in retrospection.[41] According to Black, "Matthew commonly combines καὶ with an unmarked tense-form (aorist) … reinforcing syntactical structures which guide the audience to process the following element in the discourse as continuous with that which immediately precedes."[42] In verse 25, καὶ's combination with ἠκολούθησαν, a verb in its unmarked tense-form of aorist indicative active indicates that the beginning activities of Jesus's ministry is coming to a close, showing the following of the crowd as a very important event that is related to the previous events. This interpretation is different from Kingsbury's which regards to the following of the crowd "to make Jesus the focal point of public attention."[43] For Kingsbury, the verb "to follow" distinguishes the following of the crowd from the following of the four fishermen. Kingsbury regards the following of the four fishermen as the following of disciples, but treats the following of the crowd as unimportant. My interpretation on the other hand gives attention to the crowd as a significant group made up of the various people mentioned in the unit.

---

[40] This development of the crowd character in 4:25 is based on the consideration of the crowd as a group made up of different people having diverse roles. The identity and function of the crowds have been discussed by a number of Matthean scholars. For example, Kingsbury interprets the crowd as a group of Jewish leaders. (See Jack D. Kingsbury, *The Parables of Jesus in Matthew 13: A Study in Redaction Criticism* [London: SPCK, 1978]). Van Tilborg sees the crowd differently (for Jewish leaders opposed Jesus's ministry). The crowd responds positively to Jesus's ministry (see Van Tilborg, *The Jewish Leaders*). Minear sees the crowd as "laymen of Matthew's days" (compared to the disciples as leaders; see Minear, "The Disciples and the Crowds," 28–44). Carter interprets the following of the crowd in 4:25 to show the difference between the followers that were explicitly called by Jesus and those who follow as a physical act. For Wainwright, the crowds following in 4:25 are no different from the four fishermen's following in 4:18–22 (Wainwright, *Towards a Feminist Critical Reading*, 80–81). In this way, the four fishermen are regarded as members of that crowd. Anyone from the crowd who responds to Jesus in the same way as the four fishermen, I consider *tautuatoa*.

[41] Retrospection is a repetitive device to elaborate unifying themes. It is where "the later stages of a narrative are related to what has gone before. This takes various forms in oral literature, such as summaries for recapitulation and repeated words and phrases used for characterisation." Lohr, "Oral Techniques in the Gospel of Matthew," 414.

[42] Black, *Sentence Conjunctions in the Gospel of Matthew*, 112.

[43] Kingsbury, "The Verb *AKOLOUTHEIN*," 61.

As part of the retrospection of this unit, ὄχλοι (crowds), on the one hand, invites readers to look back at the previous events involving their following of Jesus. On the other hand, it reminds readers of Jesus's appeal to different members of the crowd. From the point of view of the crowd, the arrangement of the unit develops alongside Jesus'smovement in the unit, the crowd's function in relation to Galilee and to nearby places where the impact of Jesus's ministry spreads.[44]

With the lens of *fa'asinomaga*, I see the crowd persuading readers to look back at Galilee as a place of significance. Galilee is not just the place where Jesus starts his ministry, but also where the people gathered, forming the great crowd that followed Jesus. The crowd as a rhetorical collective is formed in the local place of Galilee. Galilee is also a local place where people from outside of Galilee come to Jesus. These different groups of people have left the spaces they are familiar with in order to seek in Jesus's space help for their needs. As such, I see them as *tautuatoa*.

Summary

The analysis of the innertexture has shown that the words, narration and progression of the text may be understood in terms of how Jesus and the crowd belong to the place of Galilee. This part of the analysis shows that the purpose of Jesus's dwelling in Galilee is to proclaim ἡ βασιλεία τῶν οὐρανῶν to the Galileans and those beyond Galilee who are constructed as local people in darkness and the shadow of death. It also reveals Galilee as a local place where other people from outside of Galilee come, to seek help in Jesus's ministry. Galilee is an important local place in the narrator's telling of the beginning of Jesus's ministry.

The connection of the three parts of the rhetorical unit, from the beginning to end, displays a development of the crowd's character in conjunction with Jesus's proclamation of ἡ βασιλεία τῶν οὐρανῶν. The calling of the four fishermen, as members of the crowd, exemplifies the local people who sit in darkness but have seen a great light (4:15–16). As such, they are courageous *tautai* who, de-

---

[44] The significance of the crowd in this part of Matthew's story is that it shows the group following Jesus to be made up of Jews and gentiles. For Stanton the crowd is associated with the Matthean recitation of Isaiah's prophecy in 4:14–16. Stanton counters Anthony Saldarini's interpretation of the crowd as designation of the Jewish community in Matthew. See Anthony Saldarini, *Matthew's Christian-Jewish Community* (Chicago: University of Chicago Press, 1994), 37–40; Anthony Saldarini, "The Gospel of Matthew and Jewish-Christian Conflict," in *Social History of the Matthean Community: Cross-Discplinary Approaches*, ed. David L. Balch (Minneapolis: Fortress, 1991), 38–61; and Graham N. Stanton, "Revisiting Matthew's Communities," *HvTSt* 52 (1996): 376–94.

spite the struggle and suffering in their local place, seek ways in other spaces that will help their situations. The fishermen are shown as good examples.

Inter-textures: Isa 8:23–9:1

The intertextual analysis of Matt 4:12–25 will show how Matthew's recitation[45] of Isa 8:23–9:1 affirms Jesus's sense of belonging to Galilee, where his proclamation of ἡ βασιλεία τῶν οὐρανῶν begins. As claimed above, the reason for Jesus's dwelling in Galilee is to attend to the needs of the local people, both Jews and gentiles, who were the targeted first audience of Jesus's ministry.[46]

Matthean recitation of Isa 8:23–9:1

Matthew 4:15–16 recites Isa 8:23–9:1 (MT, but Isa 9:1–2 in the LXX).[47] I base the analysis on the MT making comparison with the LXX. I see the recitation of Isa 8:23–9:1 as having a twofold function. First, the recitation of Isa 8:23 in

---

[45] "Recitation is the transmission of speech or narrative, from either oral or written tradition, in the exact words in which the person has revealed the speech or narrative or in different words" (Robbins, *Exploring the Texture of Texts*, 41).

[46] This interpretation differs from J. Andrew Overman's argument that gentiles play no major role in Matthew (J. Andrew Overman, *Matthew's Gospel and Formative Judaism: The Social World of the Matthean Community* [Minneapolis: Fortress, 1990], 157). Douglas R. A. Hare is critical of Overman's claim saying: "this argument is faulty on at least two counts: (1) gentiles are more prominent in Matthew's gospel than in Mark's ... (2) the First Evangelist, like the Second, is writing a gospel, not a history of the early church" (Douglas R. A. Hare, "How Jewish is the Gospel of Matthew?," *CBQ* 62.2 (2000): 264–77).

Studies that consider Mathew's community as a Jewish sect that admitted gentiles in and through observation of the law include Amy-Jill Levine, *The Social and Ethnic Dimensions of Matthean Social History: "Go nowhere among the Gentiles..." (Matt. 10:5b)* (Lewiston: Edwin Mellen, 1988); and Saldarini, *Matthew's Christian-Jewish Community*.

[47] This Matthean recitation of Isa 8:23–9:1 can also be interpreted as "pesher like" or prophecy interpretation. *Pesher* is a form of interpretation in Midrash in which prophecy is used as retrospection of activities that have gone before. A *pesher* interpretation as shown in Qumran writings is an interpretation that follows after stating a prophecy. The Matthean use of the Old Testament quotations shows another way of doing *pesher* interpretation (see Bailey and Vander Broek, *Literary Forms in the New Testament*, 157–58). After telling and showing words and deeds of Jesus then come the Old Testament quotations to elaborate on the reasons for Jesus's undertakings in the story. For example, Matt 3:1–4:13 is the story of Jesus's relationship to John the Baptist in terms of the proclamation of God's βασιλεία which ends with Jesus's move to Galilee. It is followed by the narrator's use of an Old Testament quotation in Matt 4:15–16 to affirm the meaning and purpose of Jesus's withdrawal to Galilee. That is, Jesus as light withdraws to Galilee in order to shine upon the people of Galilee sitting in darkness and the shadow of death.

Matt 4:15 describes the location of the lands of Zebulun and Naphtali. Second, Matt 4:16 repeats Isa 9:1 to affirm Jesus's ministry in Galilee as a mission that did not happen by coincidence. Jesus's ministry is part of God's plan spoken in and through the prophet Isaiah.

MT (Isa 8:23)

כי לא מוצף לאשר מוצק לה כצת הראשון הקל ארצה זבלון וארצה נפתלי והאחרון הכביד
דרך הים עבר הירדן גליל הגוים:

LXX (Isa 9:1)

καὶ οὐκ ἀπορηθήσεται ὁ ἐν στενοχωρίᾳ ὢν ἕως καιροῦ τοῦτο πρῶτον ποίει ταχύ ποίει χῶρα Ζαβουλωνή γῆ Νεφθαλιμ ὁδὸν θαλάσσης καὶ οἱ λοιποὶ οἱ τὴν παραλίαν κατοικοῦντες καί πέραν τοῦ Ιορδάνου Γαλιλαία τῶν ἐθνῶν τὰ μέρητῆς Ιουδαίας

Matt 4:15

γῆ Ζαβουλὼν καὶ γῆ Νεφθαλίμ, ὁδὸν θαλάσσης, πέραν τοῦ Ἰορδάνου Γαλιλαία τῶν ἐθνῶν

NRSV

Land of Zebulun, land of Naphtali, on the road by the sea, across the Jordan, Galilee of the gentiles.

In Matt 4:15, the narrator draws the readers into Isaiah in order to provide a reason why Jesus withdraws to Capernaum. The arrangement of the rhetorical unit indicates how the recitation functions in the narration of the prologue of Jesus's ministry.

The recitation affirms the time and space where Jesus's ministry begins and the people involved in that mission. The recitation also helps make clear the function of verses 12–16 as the beginning of the first activities of Jesus's ministry, where Isa 8:23–9:1 is presented as a saying chreia.[48] The literary function of a chreia is to present a statement or action that is attributed to a particular person of importance. The Matthean narrative evokes the significance of Isaiah the prophet.

The naming of the prophet Isaiah evokes Isa 6:1–13; prophet Isaiah is the messenger sent by God when king Uzziah died and king Ahaz came to power in Judah, to announce to the people of Judah and Israel God's displeasure with their disobedience (Isa 7:1–8:22). The text presents Isaiah as a prophet with authority. As such, the Matthean reconfiguration of Isaiah brings authority to the

---

[48] George Kennedy, *Progymnasmata: Greek Textbooks of Prose Composition and Rhetoric* (Atlanta: Society of Biblical Literature, 2003), 15.

presentation of Jesus as the Messiah as well as draws the attention of the hearer/reader to Jesus's dwelling in Galilee.

Isaiah 8:23–9:1 is part of the conclusion to the unit Isa 6:1–9:7,[49] where hope of salvation is announced to the people of Israel and Judah after their encounter with disasters (the result of Israel's and Judah's disobedience; Isa 7:1–8:23). Isaiah delivers God's message to Israel and Judah—do not make allies with neighbouring nations such as Assyria. They disobey, which results in Isaiah's message of condemnation. That message ends with hope (Isa 9:1–7), which suggests that God's mercy and love upon the people of Israel continues. The lands of Zebulun and Naphtali, mentioned in Isa 8:23–9:1 as the lands of darkness and the shadow of death, experienced God's condemnation as well as the promise of the dawning of new light.

MT (Isa 9:1)

העם ההלכים בחשך ראו אור גדול ישבי בארץ צלמות אור נגה עליהם:

LXX (Isa 9:1)

ὁ λαός ὁ πορευόμενος ἐν σκότει ἴδετε φῶς μέγα οἱ κατοικοῦντες ἐν χώρα καὶ σκιᾶ θανάτου φῶς λάμψειἐφ' ὑμᾶς

Matt 4:16

ὁ λαὸς ὁ καθήμενος ἐν σκότει φῶς εἶδεν μέγα, καὶ τοῖς καθημένοις ἐν χώρα καὶ σκιᾶ θανάτου φῶς ἀνέτειλεν αὐτοῖς.

NRSV

The people who sat in darkness have seen a great light, and for those who sat in the region and shadow of death light has dawned.

The recitation of Isa 9:1 in Matt 4:16 suggests that Jesus's ministry gives hope of salvation to the people of Galilee. Matthew nonetheless makes some changes to the Isaiah text. The first change is with the MT's ההלכים (having walked; LXX: ὁπορευόμενος, having proceeded) to ὁ καθήμενος (having sat). This change links to Jesus's walk by the sea in verse 18. It contrasts those who sit in darkness from the walk of Jesus, and the message is clear: get out of sitting in darkness and the shadow of death, and walk (with Jesus) in the light. In this regard, ἡ βασιλεία τῶν οὐρανῶν requires repentance.

The other important change is Matthew's use of ἀνέτειλεν (caused to rise) which is a verb in its aorist indicative form (compare to LXX's future indicative active in λάμψει, will shine). Matthew's ἀνέτειλεν is closer to the MT's נגה (qal perfect). The aorist indicative active form expresses an event that has already

---

[49] Isa 6:1–9:7 is regarded as a distinct literary unit in the book of Isaiah. See Gene M. Tucker, *The Book of Isaiah 1–39*, NIB 6 (Nashville: Abingdon Press, 2001), 99.

been completed but whose function is still in effect, which is also the literary function of qal perfect in Hebrew. Thus, Matthew's recitation of the dawning of the light upon those walking in darkness (MT) is an event completed in the past but its function continues. The LXX's future indicative active, on the other hand, suggests that the shining of light is yet to come. Matthew's recitation thus exhibits God's dealing with the disobedient nation—God punishes Israel at the hands of its enemies and God rescues them.

The intertextual effect in Matt 4:15–16 points to Galilee's important place in God's plan of salvation. That plan started with the history of Israel and continues into the time of Jesus's ministry. Thus, Galilee is not just a place to indicate a departure point for Jesus's ministry which is aimed at its culmination in Jerusalem. Galilee as a place on its own is evoked in relation to Jesus's ministry. Through the lens of *fa'asinomaga*, Jesus is characterized as belonging to Galilee. Intertextually, Jesus's ministry in the local place of Galilee is characterized as part of God's plan to save. He makes his home in Galilee in order that the Isaiah's prophecy of salvation might be fulfillled.

Isa 8:23–9:1 as a Prophetic Message of Hope

The Matthean recitation recontextualizes Isa 8:23–9:1 as a Christian prophetic rhetorolect[50] revealing the early Christians' blending of their worlds with the prophecies of the Old Testament. The recontextualization reflects Jesus's vision of ἡ βασιλεία τῶν οὐρανῶν as a vision from a third space. This third space can be looked at in various ways. It reveals Jesus's standing in-between the spaces of being a Jew in a gentile world where he proclaims ἡ βασιλεία τῶν οὐρανῶν for both Jews and gentiles. Further, Jesus positions himself in-between being a prophet and a local Galilean where he announces to the people of Galilee the will of God. These in-between positions show his ministry as *tautuaileva* to certain people in particular places.

A prophetic announcement delivers an indictment, a request for repentance, and prophecies of promise.[51] An indictment condemns people for their disobedience to God's command; a request for repentance confirms the condemnation and offers hope of salvation, encouraging people to be obedient; the promise of salvation reveals the unconditional love of God. According to Robbins,

> a prophetic rhetorolect emerges when God decides to create a kingdom of people on earth who have special responsibility to live according to God's will. To

---

[50] "A rhetorolect or rhetorical dialect is a form of language variety or discourse identifiable on the basis of a distinctive configuration of themes, topics, reasonings, and argumentations" (Robbins, *The Invention of Christian Discourse*, 7).
[51] Walter Brueggemann, *Theology of the Old Testament: Testimony, Dispute, Advocacy* (Minneapolis: Fortress, 1997), 635–39.

initiate a special kingdom, God confronts various people with directions concerning actions God wants them to take to create this kingdom. The actions
they must undertake include confrontation of various people to communicate to
them the will of God concerning their actions, speech, and beliefs.[52]

The declaration of Jesus as Son of God in his baptism (Matt 3:16–17) reveals God-given authority to Jesus, to create in and through him the βασιλεία of
God's people on earth. And Jesus's defeat of the devil's temptation (Matt 4:1–
11) proves Jesus's messiahship. After his temptation, the narrator speaks of Jesus making his home in Galilee, and he utilises Isa 8:23–9:1 as fulfillment of
that movement. The prophecy, in the narrative context of the book of Isaiah, is a
prophecy of messianic hope of salvation. Analysing the movement of Jesus to
Galilee (4:12) in light of that prophecy, depicts Jesus as the prophet and the light
that will confront people sitting in darkness. That confrontation begins in verse
17, showing Jesus as a prophet who appeals for repentance. This not only suggests God's persistent intervention in the people's affairs but also, in the words
of Margaret Hannan, "it demands a response to God's invitation to enter into or
renew one's commitment to a relationship of faithfulness to the covenant."[53]
What this means in relation to Jesus's relationship to the crowd in Matt 4:12–25
is that Jesus's dwelling in Galilee is to help the Galileans (Jews and gentiles)
rebuild their relationship with God.

Considering Jesus's move to Galilee as a hostile action against the people
who arrested John the Baptist, the recitation of Isaiah's prophecy implies condemnation of those people. Specifically, the dawning of light upon people sitting
in darkness (Matt 4:15–16) suggests condemnation of the powers and systems
that make them sit in darkness and the shadow of death. Jesus's move to Galilee
"challenges the Roman vassal's power by asserting that there is a different reign,
God's empire."[54] There are also other powers and systems besides the Romans
in Matthew's story that make people in Galilee sit in darkness, such as some
Jewish leaders' conservatism and the first century Mediterranean society's patriarchal system. The patriarchal system is a powerful system on its own whose
implementation was asserted by Roman law.[55] Thus, the Matthean use of Isa
8:23–9:1 condemns all powers and systems which have been making the people
of Galilee live in darkness. The social and cultural analysis will elaborate on that
claim in terms of the transformation of honor from the social and cultural systems of the first century Mediterranean world to the people of Galilee.

---

[52] Robbins, *The Invention of Christian Discourse*, 219.

[53] Hannan, *The Nature and Demands*, 34.

[54] Carter, "Evoking Isaiah," 514.

[55] Michael H. Crosby, *House of Disciples: Church, Economics, and Justice in Matthew*
(Maryknoll: Orbis, 1988), 27.

Summary

The Matthean recitation of Isa 8:23–9:1 affirms Jesus's relationship to the crowd in Galilee. The recitation recontextualises Isaiah's message of salvation in light of Jesus's relationship to the people of Galilee. It features as a prophetic rhetorolect that makes known the early Christian understanding of how Jesus as the Messiah became the messenger establishing the βασιλεία of God's people in the world. That Christian understanding blends the prophecies of the Old Testament with the reality of the world that the followers of Jesus face day by day. Such blending implements the will of God from a third space—"service at in-between spaces." As a prophet, Jesus proclaims ἡ βασιλεία τῶν οὐρανῶν by confronting the people of Galilee in and through his teaching, preaching and healing. The Matthean use of Isa 8:23–9:1 affirms Jesus's ministry in Galilee as a prophetic mission.

Social and Cultural Textures: Transforming of Honor

I use the lens of *tautuatoa* to explore how the social and cultural nature of Matt 4:12–25 implies Jesus's twofold relationship to the crowd in Galilee.[56] First, it shows how Jesus gives attention to the Galileans' social and cultural needs to give honor. Second, it reveals how the positive response of the crowd to Jesus's ministry was a response of honor. Jesus gave the local people opportunities to begin from where they are situated in the local society, and to find their way out of marginalization and oppression.

Honor and shame were pivotal values of antiquity that influenced how people related to each other socially and culturally in the first century Mediterranean world.[57] They are social and cultural practices first learned in the

---

[56] According to Morten H. Jensen, Galilee in the time of Herod the Great and Herod Antipas was a calm place. For Jensen, as such, it reflects stability in Galilee. Jensen's claim is based on archaeological evidences and Josephus' non-mention of any upheavals to have taken place in Galilee (Morten H. Jensen, "Rural Galilee and Rapid Changes: An Investigation of the Socio-economic Dynamics and Developments in Roman Galilee," *Biblica* 93 [2012]: 43–67). However, he fails to include the stories of Jesus's ministry in Galilee. Sean Freyne mentions in his latest study (*Jesus, a Jewish Galilean*) the importance of studying Jesus's relationship to the place of Galilee by weighing up the archaeological evidences and the four evangelists' stories. See also Halvor Moxnes, "Identity in Jesus' Galilee—From Ethnicity to Locative Intersectionality," *BibInt* 18.4–5 (2010): 390–416. In light of those studies, I acknowledge that my analysis is rhetorical rather than historical—I am not making claims about the historical Jesus.

[57] In the first century Mediterranean society, the person with honor had high status in the government. He or she had abundance of land and was born to an elite family. People receive and achieve honor when their worth and standing are acknowledged in public. (See David A. deSilva, *Honor, Patronage, Kinship and Purity: Unlocking New Testa-*

family unit but were carried into all other levels and spaces of society. Robbins writes that

> early Christian wisdom rhetorolect moves toward its goal ("to produce the fruit of goodness and righteousness in the world") by blending together human experiences of the household, the geophysical world within God's cosmos, and the intersubjective body in which people live.[58]

The analysis that follows looks at the social and cultural nature of the text to determine Jesus's ascribed and acquired honor as the foundation of honor and shame in the household of ἡ βασιλεία τῶν οὐρανῶν.

Jesus, with ascribed honor

Jesus is presented as a person with ascribed honor in the Matthean story. He comes from the Davidic line which qualifies him as a messiah according to the prophecies of Israel's prophets.[59] That messianic honor is reinforced by the angel declaring him as Immanuel to Joseph (Matt 1:18–25), by the three magi's acknowledgment and recognition of Jesus as king of the Jews (Matt 2:1–13), by God's declaration of Jesus as his son in the baptism (Matt 3:1–17), by Jesus's victory over the devil's temptation (Matt 4:1–10), and finally by the angels that waited upon Jesus (Matt 4:11). These references demonstrate Jesus's ascribed honor giving him the authority to undertake God's mission. But Jesus's ascribed honor was not recognized by other characters.

In the first century Mediterranean world, one's honor became acceptable when acknowledged and recognized publicly.[60] Thus, Jesus's ascribed honor had to become acquired honor. In other words, for the people to accept his proclamation of ἡ βασιλεία τῶν οὐρανῶν, Jesus needed to acquire the honor of being the

---

ment Culture [Downers Grove: Intervarsity, 2000], 23–94; John H. Elliott, *What Is Social-Scientific Criticism?* [Minneapolis: Fortress, 1993], 130, 133–34).

Shame is the reverse of honor. Despite the sense of negativity entailed in shame, it was accepted in the Mediterranean world (Halvor Moxnes, "Honor and Shame," in *The Social Sciences and New Testament Interpretation*, ed. Richard Rohrbaugh, 31–33). For example, a woman's place was private and her role was considered to carry shame. Being shameful in that sense was seen as normal (Moxnes, "Honor and Shame," 21–22).

For the loss of honor in relation to loss of wealth, see Jerome Neyrey, "Loss of Wealth, Loss of Family and Loss of Honor: The Cultural Context of the Original Makarisms in Q," in *Modelling Early Christianity: Social-Scientific Studies of the New Testament in Its Context*, ed. Philip E. Esler (New York: Routledge, 1995), 139–58.

[58] Robbins, *The Invention of Christian Discourse*, 121.

[59] See Jerome H. Neyrey, *Honor and Shame in the Gospel of Matthew* (Louisville: Westminster John Knox, 1998), 37.

[60] See Elliott, *What Is Social-Scientific Criticism?*, 130, 133–34.

one to do that task. Jesus must publicly demonstrate his authority to undertake that mission. The language of this text shows the Matthean presentation as a Christian wisdom rhetorolect. It is where Jesus's dwelling in Galilee is told and shown as a blending of early Christian understanding of household wisdom with Jesus's proclamation of ἡ βασιλεία τῶν οὐρανῶν as a proclamation of the household of God on earth.

Household wisdom in first century Mediterranean society was learned from participating in the dominant social and cultural system, the patriarchal system, that ran and controlled that society.[61] This social system holds the father as the head of the family who exhibits unquestioned authority over the family. This is linked to the Roman imperial power, where the Emperor was the patriarch and everyone under him are his children, thus providing the imperial system with an ideological justification to control them all.[62] In this way, those close to the Emperor have honor.

However, Jesus's withdrawal to Galilee transforms the sense of imperial honor in the first century Mediterranean world to the household system of God. This is reflected in Good's interpretation of Jesus's withdrawal to Capernaum to fulfill the prophecy in Matt 4:15–16.[63] According to that prophecy, Galilee is the place where Jesus will begin the work of salvation. Thus, honor in the household system of God is receiving salvation in and through ἡ βασιλεία τῶν οὐρανῶν.

Jesus transforms honor in light of ἡ βασιλεία τῶν οὐρανῶν

Jesus's ministry in the first part of Matthew is not a violent or aggressive resistance of political, social, and cultural systems that govern and control the local world of Galilee. Rather, it is a ministry that deals with how the local people in and through their acceptance of Jesus's proclamation of ἡ βασιλεία τῶν οὐρανῶν resist those systems.

According to the prophecy (Matt 4:15–16), Galilee is a place of darkness and the shadow of death. Jesus was the light to illuminate Galilee so that it becomes a place of honor. Thus, the honor of the household of ἡ βασιλεία τῶν οὐρανῶν is acquired by those sitting in darkness and the shadow of death in Galilee. Jerome Neyrey's consideration of the Matthean narrative as an encomium asserts the importance of Galilee as the place of honor.[64] For Neyrey, Galilee was an honourable place.[65]

---

[61] See Crosby, *House of Disciples*, 26–27; Diane Jacobs-Malina, *Beyond Patriarchy: The Images of Family in Jesus* (New York: Paulist Press, 1993), 1–2.

[62] Carter, *Matthew and Empire*, 9–34.

[63] Good, "The Verb ΑΝΑΧΩΡΕΩ," 1.

[64] Neyrey, *Honor and Shame*, 90.

[65] For a description of Galilee as a domestic space in the time of Jesus, see Moxnes, *Putting Jesus in His Place*, 38–43.

In the first century Mediterranean social and cultural world, one way of claiming honor is through challenge-response debate in public.[66] This is where "messages are transferred from a source (challenger) to a receiver."[67] After Jesus made his home in Galilee, he then moved on to appeal for repentance. It is Jesus's public appeal for repentance that is a challenge to the honor of the people of Galilee. The challenge is presented in the form of a command: *Repent for the kingdom of heaven has come near.* The announcement is delivered in deliberative language[68] with an epideictic sense[69] revealing that the people who repent will receive honor, but those who do not repent will not receive any honor.

According to Aristotle, a deliberative speech is a speech that points to the future. It is a speech to encourage the audience to do good things and to discourage the listeners from doing bad things. This is reflected in Jesus's first announcement of ἡ βασιλεία τῶν οὐρανῶν as an imperative. It reveals the coming of ἡ βασιλεία τῶν οὐρανῶν as well as how it is to be received by the people of Galilee. This deliberative speech entails an epideictic message and as such it contains a language of praise and blame.[70] Aristotle writes that in delivering an epideictic speech,

> incidentally the orator will be able to produce a certain impression as to his own moral character, the ethical kind of proof.[71]

The Matthean use of the rhetoric of praise and blame presents Jesus as ethical, emotional, and logical.[72] Jesus's ethical character is evident in his

---

[66] Robbins, *Exploring the Texture of Texts*, 80. See also Neyrey, *Honor and Shame*, 44–52.

[67] Robbins, *Exploring the Texture of Texts*, 80.

[68] Aristotle writes that "there are three kinds of rhetoric (1) deliberative; (2) forensic; (3) epideictic," for which he explains: "The business of the deliberative kind is to exhort or dissuade, its time the future, its end the expedient or the harmful: of the forensic to accuse or defend, its time the past, its end the just or the unjust; of the epideictic praise and blame, its time the present (sometimes the past of the future), its end the noble or the disgraceful" (Aristotle, *Art of Rhetoric*, xxxvii).

[69] An epideictic speech is an expression of praise and blame (Aristotle, *Art of Rhetoric*, xxxvii).

[70] The first century writers who studied ancient rhetoric in Greek learned to write events, histories and stories using different components of progymnasmata. (Progymnasmata is where a student learns the compositions in writing such as styles and forms of compositions. See Kennedy, *Progymnasmata*, ix–xiv.) One of its main elements is the rhetoric of praise and blame. This method of writing was commonly used in the Mediterranean world, and understanding the rhetoric of praise and blame in the text will give us understanding of the social and cultural topic of honor and shame in the Mediterranean world.

[71] Aristotle, *Art of Rhetoric*, xxxviii.

characterisation as Son of God (cf. 3:17) whose honor is recognized publicly by the crowds following him (4:18–25). Jesus's emotional character is seen in his moving away from his family, and his logical character is seen in the use of prophecy to underpin his teaching and healing ministry in Matt 4:15–16. Thus, Jesus's ethical, emotional, and logical characteristics make him deserving of praise and honor.

The command to repent comes with praise and blame. The word "repent" suggests that in doing so one will be praised, whereas the one who does not will be blamed. The way to claim honor is repentance. This announcement implies that the people who are called to repent are in the place of shame because of their sins. The importance of ἡ βασιλεία τῶν οὐρανῶν as an epideictic speech should be reflected in the life and character of the speaker. This is why it is important to consider that speech in relation to the speaker's life in the past. Jesus as the speaker stresses the importance of the message.

The fishermen rise to the challenge with an immediate response, leaving everything to follow Jesus.[73] As a result, the fishermen received God's honor. The status of fishermen in the first century Mediterranean context is debatable but from what can be determined from the text[74] their use of nets and boats suggests that they were commercial fishermen.[75] They would have had to pay taxes, placing them under the Roman imperial system. Also, as commercial fishermen they supply markets in other places, which sometimes are governed by patron-client relationships[76] where the fishermen are clients to the patron who was usu-

---

[72] Aristotle writes that "artificial proof in rhetoric has three kinds; (1) ethical, derived from the moral character of the speaker; (2) emotional, the object of which is to put the hearer into a certain frame of mind; (3) logical, contained in the speech itself when a real or apparent truth is demonstrated" (*Art of Rhetoric*, xxxvi).

[73] Robbins, *Exploring the Texture of Texts*, 80: "gift-giving, invitations to dinner... arranging what we might call cooperative ventures for farming, business, fishing, mutual help—all these sorts of interaction take place according to patterns of honor called challenge-response."

[74] Interpretations of fishermen as people of lesser status: K. C. Hanson and Douglas E. Oakman, *Palestine in the Time of Jesus* (Minneapolis: Fortress, 1998), 106–10 and K. C. Hanson, "The Galilean Fishing Economy and the Jesus Tradition," *BTB* 27.3 (1997): 99–111. Interpretations of fishing business as showing economic stability and secure lifestyle: Daniel J. Harrington, *The Gospel of Matthew*, Sacra Pagina (Collegeville: Liturgical Press, 2007), 72. Davies and Allison, *A Critical and Exegetical Commentary Matthew I–VII*, 397, and Jerome Murphy-O'Connor, "Fishers of Fish, Fishers of Men," *BRev* 15.3 (1999): 22–49.

[75] If the two sets of fishermen brothers were working under a lease agreement, their immediate response to follow Jesus shows their abandoning of that lease agreement.

[76] For explanations on the patron-client relationship see John J. Pilch and Bruce J. Malina eds., *Handbook of Biblical Social Values* (Peabody: Hendrickson,1980), 151–55; Neyrey, *Honor and Shame*, 37–39, 47–48, 108–14, 156–61.

ally in government. Such structures and processes can place the fishermen in the realm of shame, which was not necessarily negative. In other words, for the fishermen, "shame" was culturally accepted in the Mediterranean world. In this regard, several fishermen will never be able to reach the status of honor ascribed and acquired by those in power, some of whom were their patrons.

Jesus called the second set of brothers while they were sitting and mending their nets with their father (Matt 4:21). This suggests that fishing for them was a family affair. The appearance of the father evokes in the social and cultural texture the patriarchal system. The father was at the place of honor in the family, and he has authority over the nets, boats and fishermen. The appearance of two sets of brothers reminds the reader of how the patriarchal system controls and runs all levels of the social and cultural world of first century Mediterranean society.

If fishing is the main source of income for their families, why did the brothers leave their fishing nets, father, and boats, in order to follow Jesus? Did they leave all those behind in search of equality in Galilee? This seems unlikely. Considering the shame associated with their location on the margins of society, survival would have been more important for them. Thus, leaving their fishing gear and following Jesus reflect their seeking other ways to ensure their survival with their families.

As fishermen, they had no power and authority to resist the Roman imperial system which required them to pay taxes. The text implies that resisting those in power was not the answer. Rather, dealing with their place in the Galilean society was the starting point for emerging from the margins of society. The four men were fishermen, and Jesus was to train them to be fishermen. There is another type of fishing that will help them fulfill their tasks, and this will be done in a group of "brothers." According to Duling, forming that group is reflected in the features of "'brotherhood' language, related disciplinary processes and scribal leadership."[77]

A brotherhood[78] as a voluntary association in the first century Mediterranean world is an egalitarian group made up of various people regardless of status. Duling writes that the organization of these brotherhood associations was in

---

[77] Dennis Duling, "The Matthean Brotherhood and Marginal Scribal Leadership," in *Modelling Early Christianity: Social-Scientific Studies of the New Testament in its Context*, ed. Philip F. Esler (London: Routledge, 1995), 159.

[78] In the first century Mediterranean world, the household exhibits the patriarchal system model and brotherhood represents egalitarianism. My consideration of brotherhood in Matthew's story in conjunction with the household of God is based on regarding God as the head of that household. See also Karl Olav Sandnes, "Equality Within Patriarchal Structures: Some New Testament perspectives on the Christian fellowship as a brother- or sisterhood and family," in *Constructing Early Christian Families: Family as Social Reality and Metaphor*, ed. Halvor Moxnes (London: Routledge, 1997), 150–65.

accordance with the household system where respect was given to elders and leaders. Michael Crosby also speaks of the significance of voluntary association in the first century Mediterranean world and he mentions egalitarianism as the main principle of voluntary associations which stresses the recognition of women.[79] I see the second set of brother's leaving their father to set up a brotherhood association. This will not be in accordance with the patriarchal system that runs and controls local families but, with an alternative system where respected brothers and sisters who have wisdom will guide the association, in accordance with God's will. In leaving behind their father, the fishermen anticipate entering into the brotherhood system that will ensure their survival.

The text lacks any reference to the disciples returning home, but there is a possibility that the followers of Jesus did not abandon their families for good. According to Craig Keener's sociorhetorical interpretation, if we look at Jesus's ministry of discipleship as a seasonal ministry, it is possible that the disciples returned to their families for parts of the year.[80] Agrarian workers could afford to be away from sowing and harvesting but for a fisherman to be away from fishing for a long period of time was costly for the family. Keener also shows that weather conditions stopped people from making long distance travel. For those reasons, "while disciples undoubtedly spent some nights away from home (especially when they traversed the lake), the gospel itineraries suggest that they often ministered within walking distance of Capernaum."[81] Following Jesus by abandoning one's family is not the only way to understand the fishermen's response to Jesus's call.

J. Andrew Overman speaks against assuming that the disciples did not return home. According to Overman, "one could easily travel with Jesus for several days, or even one day, get to a Galilean town, engage in an argument with local leaders, and be home by nightfall."[82] In considering these reasons there is "a different picture of the relationship between Jesus's movement and their native region, Lower Galilee."[83] Leaving one's family to follow Jesus without return is not a compelling characteristic of following Matthew's Jesus. Both Keener and Overman argue from a historical perspective but their conclusions can be drawn into an interpretation of the sociocultural texture of the text. This is evident in Jesus's relationship to the people of Galilee (Matt 4:12–25). The immediate response of the brothers suggests that they were willing to help

---

[79] Crosby, *House of Disciples*, 30–36.

[80] Craig S. Keener, *The Gospel of Matthew: A Socio-rhetorical Commentary* (Grand Rapids: Eerdmans, 2009), 148–55.

[81] Ibid., 153.

[82] J. Andrew Overman, *Church and Community in Crisis: The Gospel according to Matthew* (Pennsylvania: Trinity Press International, 1996), 67.

[83] Ibid.

anyone in need in Galilee including their families, and Jesus was leading the way. Leaving the nets, boats and father implies that they were ready to abandon the patron-client relationship and patriarchal system they have been part of, in order to become members of the brotherhood association.

Becoming a member of the brotherhood group brings one into a patron-client relationship. In Matt 4, Jesus is the broker in-between God (patron) and the people of Galilee (clients). Jesus as broker puts forward to the people of Galilee the challenge of repentance as the way to obtain honor in ἡ βασιλεία τῶν οὐρανῶν. Thus, every one from Galilee has opportunity to gain honor in the household of God if they accept Jesus's proclamation.

In verses 23–25, the narrator tells how the brotherhood is to be formed through the teaching, preaching, and proclamation of ἡ βασιλεία τῶν οὐρανῶν. The sick are socially and religiously marginalized, indicating the failure of the social, cultural and religious systems in Galilee. As such, Jesus's healing of the sick goes beyond the physical remedy of the body. It is holistic healing of the body, mind, soul and spirit.[84] Jesus gave primary attention to these people, and the outcome is that they became part of Galilean society again. In doing so, and in a similar respect to his interaction with the fishermen in Matt 4:12–25, Jesus gave them the honor of ἡ βασιλεία τῶν οὐρανῶν.

With the lens of *fa'asinomaga*, repentance was the honorable way to become a better Galilean. The fishermen were the first people from Galilee to have received that honor. The positive responses of the fishermen to Jesus's ministry, and of other members of the crowd such as the sick, made them *tautuatoa*. These are local people from Galilee who take the risk of following and believing in Jesus's ministry in the midst of the colonialist social, cultural, political, and religious systems that ran and controlled Galilee.

Summary

The social and cultural analysis showed that Jesus attends first to the social and cultural needs and rights of the local Galileans. It demonstrated a reversal of

---

[84] Wainwright's interpretation of Jesus's healing of women in Matthew's gospel reflects Jesus's healing approach as holistic and wholistic in which the participation of the sick as the healed is important. See Elaine M. Wainwright, "'Your Faith Has Made You Well'. Jesus, Women, and Healing in the Gospel of Matthew," in *Transformative Encounters: Jesus and Women Re-viewed*, ed. Ingrid Rosa Kitzberger (Leiden: Brill, 2000), 224–45; Wainwright, *Towards a Feminist Critical Reading*, 83–95; 98–117. In a comparison of Jesus's healing ministry in the New Testament to Traditional and Christian Samoan healing practices, Otele Perelini points out that one of the similarities of those healing activities is the use of the holistic approach where the healing is looked upon beyond the physical remedy of the body. See Otele Perelini, "A Comparison of Jesus' Healing with Healing in Traditional and Christian Samoa" (PhD Dissertation, Edinburgh University, 1992).

honor in light of Jesus's proclamation of ἡ βασιλεία τῶν οὐρανῶν to the people of Galilee. This analysis explored the social and cultural textures of Matt 4:12–25 as a Christian wisdom rhetorolect that presents Jesus's dwelling in Galilee as establishing the household of God in which honor is given to the members of the crowd who repent and follow Jesus. Furthermore, Jesus called the fishermen to form a voluntary association of brotherhood whose aim and purpose was to give primary attention to the needs and rights of the local people in Galilee.

Conclusion

With the hermeneutic of *tautuaileva*, I read Matt 4:12–25 as a *siomiaga fa'atusiga* (rhetorical and narrative unit) that demonstrates how and why Galilee as a local place was significant in the beginning of the Matthean account of Jesus's ministry.

Through the lens of *fa'asinomaga*, I showed in the innertextual and intertextual analyses the connection of Jesus and the crowd to Galilee. The beginning of Jesus's ministry in Galilee was part of God's plan to restore the Jews as well as the gentiles.

Through the lens of *tautuatoa*, I saw the development of Jesus's relationship to the crowd in and through the language, narration, and progression of Matt 4:12–25 to reveal local people going beyond common spaces to seek ways to help them move away from the margin of society. That view was developed further through the lens of *tautuatoa* in the social and cultural textual analysis, in which I saw Jesus's ministry as an honorable service that gave honor to those in need. The members from the crowd who responded positively to that ministry acquired honor. The egalitarianism in Jesus's vision of ἡ βασιλεία τῶν οὐρανῶν gives the disadvantaged a way out of oppression.

My *tautuaileva* analysis of Matt 4:12–25 has shown that discipleship is not a global-based ministry. Rather, discipleship is a local place-based mission. The growth of discipleship as a mission is measured by the consideration of the needs and rights of local people in a local place.

5.
TAUTUAILEVA READING OF MATTHEW 7:24–8:22

This chapter analyses Matt 7:24–8:22 for how Jesus's ministry to a local place (Galilee) reveals his attention to the needs and rights of local people.[1] The analysis will focus on the person in need, in accordance with the situation in which s/he is caught.

What do the literary features of Matt 7:24–8:22, as *siomiaga fa'atusiga* (a rhetorical and narrative unit), show about Jesus's ministry to local households? How do those demonstrate Jesus's attention to the needs and rights of local people? What is Jesus's sense of belonging to Galilee? What do the literary features of this text reveal about the crowd, their link to local households, and their sense of belonging to Galilee? What do the literary features of the text show about Jesus and the crowd as *tautuatoa*?

Matt 7:24–8:22 as Rhetorical and Narrative Unit (*siomiaga fa'atusiga*)

In seeking to establish Matt 7:24–8:22 as a rhetorical unit, I acknowledge at the outset that this unit cuts across some of the scholarly positions concerning narrative or rhetorical units. Hence the need to argue for the unit, starting with a discussion of B. W. Bacon's (traditional) structuring of Matthew.

Bacon focuses on the alternation of narrative and discourse material in Matthew.[2] His structure considers chapter 7 as part of the discourse (Sermon on the Mount from chapters 5–7) and chapter 8 as part of the narrative (healings and miracles in chapters 8–9). There are five discourses in this structure, each marked by the formulaic saying, *Now when Jesus had finished saying these things.* Despite Bacon seeing chapters 7 and 8 in separate sections, other scholars, including D. A. Hagner and Robert H. Gundry, read Matt 8 and 9 with the Sermon on the Mount. These chapters tell and show the authority of Jesus as Messiah.[3] Gundry speaks of the connection between the deeds and words of

---

[1] Parts of this chapter will be published as "Jesus the *Fiaola* (Opportunity Seeker): A Hybrid Samoan Reading of Matthew 8:1–17," in *Sea of Readings: The Bible and the South Pacific Islands*, ed. Jione Havea (Atlanta: SBL Press, forthcoming).

[2] See, Bauer, *The Structure of Matthew's Gospel*, 21–56.

[3] Hagner, *Matthew 1–13*, 195.

Jesus in chapters 5–9 which assert Jesus's authority.[4] These are, however, more thematic than rhetorical links.

According to the *tautuaileva* hermeneutic (chapters 2 and 3), one's sense of belonging to a place is revealed in words and in deeds. Thus, my selection of Matt 7:24–8:22 as a rhetorical and narrative unit cuts across some of the traditional and textual elements of Matthew. One of these is the formulaic saying in Matt 7:28 which indicates the end of the Sermon on the Mount. I have nonetheless chosen to read Matt 7:24–8:22 as a rhetorical unit because it is Matthew's telling and showing of Jesus's relationship to the crowd according to their interactions in words and actions.

In chapter three, I argued that identity is not just about identifying the person according to the culture to which s/he belongs, but also how s/he puts that culture into practice. Thus, one's sense of belonging to a place is action-in-progress where one relates to other people in ways that are shaped by the changes s/he encounters in that place. In this way, Jesus's relationship to the crowd, will be identified and explored in terms of their words and actions. My consideration of Matt 7:24–8:22 as a rhetorical unit emphasizes Jesus's relationship to different households in that unit. Through the *tautuaileva* hermeneutic, Jesus's use of the imagery of building a house in the parable of the wise and the fool (Matt 7:24–27) anticipates his healing of sick people from different households in Matt 8:1–17. In the progression of the unit, Jesus's movement towards local households, which culminates in a transition of movement from one side of the sea to the other, is anticipated in Matt 8:18–22. I will elaborate on this interpretation below, based on the following structure:

> Matt 7:24–29 *Amataga* (Beginning): Discipleship as re-building
> Matt 8:1–17 *Ogatotonu* (Middle): Discipleship as healing
> Matt 8:18–22 *Faaiuga* (End): Jesus commands continuation of discipleship

Opening and closing signs of the rhetorical unit

Matthew 7:24–8:22 has opening and closing signs that form an *inclusio*. These signs direct the reader to local factors in the text, which exhibit the rhetorical place as Galilee. I find the following four opening and closing signs in the unit.

First, attention is drawn to the conjunctions in the first (7:24) and last (8:22) verses which indicate the opening and closing of the rhetorical unit. The use of the conjunction οὖν (then) in 7:24 not only signals the end of Jesus's Sermon on the Mount but it also directs the audience to a new description of the true hearer of his words. I view the characteristics of this type of hearer (listening and acting), as described in the image of house building, as characteristics of a local

---

[4] See Robert H. Gundry, *Matthew: A Commentary on His Handbook for a Mixed Church under Persecution*, 2nd ed. (Grand Rapids: Eerdmans, 1994), 137.

person as servant who belongs to a local household. In her study of the use of conjunctions in Matthew, Black describes the use of οὖν "as a signal ...of continuation and retrospect."[5] She adds that οὖν as a "procedural signal guide[s] the audience to integrate additional material into the narrative discourse, or rather, into the mental representations which [it] construct[s] of the discourse."[6] As such, οὖν in 7:24 signals transition from ἡ βασιλεία τῶν οὐρανῶν (the emphasis of the Sermon on the Mount, 5:3–7:23), to its application (beginning at 7:24). That application tells the audience what to do with Jesus's teaching in their local settings. In the last verse of the unit, 8:22, the conjunction δὲ (but) indicates that the unit comes to an end, but with the sense of continuation to a different set of events. It indicates that the unit ends with leaving the household and following Jesus. The conjunction also suggests continuation of the story, as shown in Jesus's dealing with demons on the other side of the sea beginning in 8:23.

Second, through the *fa'asinomaga* lens, I see the beginning (7:24–29) and ending (8:18–22) as signs of Jesus belonging to the local households. The beginning (7:24–29) includes Jesus's explanation of listening with actions, as his way of dealing with people. This reflects the narrator's knowledge and understanding of the local place.[7] In Michael Crosby's consideration of οἰκία/οἶκος (house) as an "assumed primary metaphor," he argues that "οἰκία/οἶκος are not just words; they represent an entire cultural referent, a world of meaning."[8] He adds that "without the house, church and economics did not exist at the time when Jesus lived and Matthew wrote."[9] In Matthew, "house" is a metaphor that represents a particular local world (Galilee) in terms of its social, cultural, economic, political, and religious values and systems.[10] That function of "house" is reflected in the parable of the wise and fool building houses. Jesus spoke of building a house with the local natural materials of rock and sand, as symbols for building upon the ways of God.

In the conclusion of the unit (8:18–22), Jesus's responses to the scribe (8:20) and to one of his disciples (8:22) reflect his knowledge and understanding of the local space. He understood the local fauna, and compared it to his not having a house or a home to rest. Here, Jesus used the house built by foxes to elucidate the kind of discipleship he proposes. His reply to one of his disciples

---

[5] Black, *Sentence Conjunctions*, 273.

[6] Ibid., 260.

[7] On the landscape and weather conditions of this local place, see Arland J. Hultgren, *The Parables of Jesus: A Commentary* (Grand Rapids: Eerdmans, 2000), 133.

[8] Crosby, *House of Disciples*, 10.

[9] Ibid., 11.

[10] According to John Elliott, οἶκος was the primary basis for the Christian movement in the first century where Christians learned the reality of life in terms of their social, political, economic, religious and moral values. John H. Elliott, *A Home for the Homeless: A Sociological Exegesis of 1 Peter, Its Situation and Strategy* (London: SCM, 1982), 213.

shows another type of household that needs rebuilding, namely, the family. These images of different households, exhibited at the beginning and end of the unit, provide a picture of the locality of Jesus's ministry.

Third, through the lens of *tautuatoa*, I find a courageous Jesus moving from familiar to unfamiliar relationships in 7:24–8:22. Jesus was the one with power and authority in the relationship with the crowd (the Πᾶς [everyone] that Jesus addressed in 7:24). In 7:28, the crowd marvel at Jesus's teaching, which indicates Jesus's authority.[11] As the narrative unfolds, the crowd's character is important not only as the witness to Jesus's ministry, but also as the character whose relationship to Jesus demonstrates the purpose of Jesus's ministry. That purpose is to serve the needs and rights of local people. In the conclusion of the unit (8:18–22), Jesus ordered the crowd to go over to the other side thereby gesturing his authority once more. He told them what to do. Go!

In the beginning of the unit, the scribes do not have the authority that Jesus has (7:29). In the closing of the unit, the scribe's request to follow Jesus shows the authority of Jesus which is manifested in the healing events in the middle of the unit (8:1–17). Jesus leads the ministry of attending to the needs of the local people. According to the *tautuaileva* hermeneutic, anyone who has connections to a local family, household, and community, is a servant because s/he has a service role to play as a member of that family, household, and community. As such, I see the signs of Jesus's relationship to the crowd as showing that he was a servant.

Fourth, Matt 7:24 and 8:22 are rhetorical signs of Jesus calling the crowd to his ministry. In the lens of *tautuatoa*, a local family member is a servant who has subjectivity (*loto fuatiaifo*) and agency to carry out his/her service role. Jesus's telling the crowd of the type of listener he expects in 7:24 indicates how a local person should have the initiative in carrying out that role in-between familiar and unfamiliar spaces. In 7:24 Jesus says, "Πᾶς οὖν ὅστις ἀκούει μου τοὺς λόγους τούτους καὶ ποιεῖ αὐτοὺς" (Everyone who hears these words of mine and does them) and in 8:22 he utters, "Ἀκολούθειμοι" (Follow me)—the latter is a plea for continuation of the type of discipleship for which Jesus called. Both verses state some of the characteristics of becoming Jesus's disciple, namely, to follow Jesus by listening to his teaching and doing them.

---

[11] The reading proposed in this chapter considers the crowd as the main audience and the disciples are part of that group. This is based on Matt 5:1 where both crowd and disciples are mentioned: "When Jesus saw the crowds, he went up the mountain; and after he sat down, his disciples came to him" (it is here that the word "disciple" is first mentioned in Matthew's story). When he saw the crowd, he went up the mountain to find a good place from where to deliver his speech so that everyone in the crowd could hear him. It is after he sat down that the disciples came to him. This suggests that the disciples were not a separate group from the crowd but listeners who emerge from the crowd. Thus, the main audience is the crowd from whom the listeners to Jesus's ministry should emerge.

These opening and closing signs are rhetorical frames that show, in and through Jesus's relationship to the crowd, the type of discipleship emphasised in Matt 7:24–8:22. According to the *tautuaileva* hermeneutic, this is a place-based discipleship that gives primary attention to the needs of local people. Matthew 8:1–17 (the middle segment of the unit) unpacks that type of discipleship.

Rhetorical Arrangement of Matt 7:24–8:22

The rhetorical arrangement of 7:24–8:22 presents two important developments that reveal discipleship as a local place-based ministry, and an undertaking of *tautuatoa*. First is in Jesus entering local household space. Jesus's ministry is a ministry to local families and households. Second is in the local people listening to, and act upon, Jesus's proclamation of ἡ βασιλεία τῶν οὐρανῶν.

With respect to the first development: In the beginning of the unit (7:24–29), Jesus speaks of the type of listening he expects in relation to building a house. The kind of builder Jesus prefers is a *tufuga* who is prepared to go beyond listening into action. The kind of action Jesus targeted is the (re)building of local families and households. Jesus shows how this is to be carried out in 8:1–17: there is a pattern here in the contraction of space, in the progression of the healing events from the healing of the leper to the healing of Peter's mother-in-law.[12] In the healing of the leper (8:1–4), there is no reference to a house. In the healing of the centurion's servant, Jesus stood not far from the centurion's house. And in the healing of Peter's mother-in-law, Jesus enters a local house. In the progression of these stories, Jesus moves toward and enters a local house. Matthew 8:17 (reciting Isa 53:4) shows why this type of ministry is important: because it helps to carry away the sufferings of members in need. The unit ends (8:18–22) with Jesus leaving the local household and moving on to the next part of his ministry.

For the second development: In Matt 7:24–8:22 also, Jesus shows another form of what it means for local people to listen—they are to enter unfamiliar spaces to deal with their needs. This too is about hearing Jesus's teachings and acting. It exhibits subjectivity to seek other ways or opportunities available in the local world. Matthew 7:24–8:22 is arranged into these parts: introduction, statement of the case, proofs, and conclusion.[13] The introduction explains the combination of listening and doing. Jesus's words "Everyone who hears these words of mine and does them" state the expectation. Jesus the speaker is represented in the possessive pronoun μου (of my), which shows that his words are

---

[12] Healing of Peter's mother-in-law presents Jesus as prophet in a way similar to healing stories in the Old Testament, e.g., Elisha's healing the Shunammite woman's son in 2 Kings 4:18–37 (see Wilson, "The Uninvited Healer," 53–72).

[13] These as a pattern of argumentation, see Mack, *Rhetoric*, 41–48; Kennedy, *New Testament Interpretation*, 23–24.

useful to the people of the local place—the crowd. The statement in 7:24 also refers to the crowd as the audience with the adjective πᾶς (every one) indicating inclusivity.

The proposition of the unit is listening to, and acting upon, Jesus's proclamation of ἡ βασιλεία τῶν οὐρανῶν. This is elaborated in the parable of the wise and the fool in 7:24–27 and the response of the crowd in 7:28–29. Its function as Hultgren observes is "to move hearers of the Sermon to contemplate what has been said and to act upon the teachings of Jesus."[14] This proposition is made clearer by the contrast between the imagery of building the house on rock, and building the house on sand. The person who built his house on the rock is the wise listener while the person who built his house on the sand is the fool. Becoming the wise or foolish builder is determined by how the houses stand against the winds and the rains. After the narrator presents Jesus's words to the crowd (7:24–27), the narrative then moves on to the reliability and authority of Jesus as the speaker in 7:24–27. This is shown in an enthymeme in 7:28–29:

Καὶ ἐγένετο ὅτε ἐτέλεσεν ὁ Ἰησοῦς τοὺς λόγους τούτους ἐξεπλήσσοντο οἱ ὄχλοι ἐπὶ τῇ διδαχῇ αὐτοῦ ἦν **γὰρ** διδάσκων αὐτοὺς ὡς ἐξουσίαν ἔχων καὶ οὐχ ὡς οἱ γραμματεῖς αὐτῶν.

Now when Jesus finished saying these things, the crowds were astounded at his teaching, **for** he taught them as one having authority, and not as their scribes.

In this enthymeme, verse 28 presents the statement and verse 29 provides the supporting reason signalled by the conjunction γὰρ (for). The statement indicates that Jesus's sermon is now finished and the crowd responds with amazement. The crowd's astonishment was because Jesus was "teaching with authority."[15] The enthymeme affirms the credibility of Jesus's sermon. As such, what is contained in the speech is not to be ignored. It persuades the hearers and readers to also listen to the next part of the story, for the authority of Jesus. Jesus will show that "listening with actions" will help local people in distress. This is the way of a *tautuatoa*.

Listening with actions begins in 8:1–4 and continues to 8:17, with Jesus healing different members of the crowd. The positive response of the crowd

---

[14] Hultgren, *The Parables*, 132.

[15] According to Cousland, the crowds "do not move beyond their initial amazement either to appropriate Jesus's teaching or to reject him. They remained static and uncommitted either way." J. R. C. Cousland, *The Crowds in the Gospel of Matthew*, NovTSup 102 (Leiden: Brill, 2002), 128. Cousland further said that such crowd's level of understanding of Jesus's ministry makes 7:28–29 as "the prelude" to a thematic interpretation of the crowd in the gospel. In my *tautuaileva* reading, I extend the textual section to 7:24 (with 7:24–8:22 is a rhetorical unit) thus pushing back what counts as the prelude.

affirms the message Jesus preached for the local people to deal with their needs. Matthew's recitation of Isa 53:4 in Matt 8:17 marks the end of this section. In 8:18, having seen that the crowd size is growing, Jesus orders them to go over to the other side, indicating that the rhetorical unit is coming to a conclusion (8:18–22).

The arrangement of Matt 7:24–8:22 shows, with the metaphor of building a house, how Jesus deals with various members of the crowd. He (re)built local households in and through listening and doing. Discipleship is giving attention to the needs of members of the crowd from different local households. The Matthean blending of the household of God (in ἡ βασιλεία τῶν οὐρανῶν) with local households in Galilee has to do with meeting the needs and rights of the poor and marginalized. The following analysis expands on this observation.

Inner-textures: Fa'asinomaga and Tautuatoa

This analysis is twofold. First, through the lens of *fa'asinomaga*, because Jesus teaches the crowd how to listen through house building, I see every member of the crowd as belonging to a "household" (*aiga*).[16] I identify the households as familiar local dwelling spaces to which certain members of the crowd belong, and their roles within these households. Second, through the lens of *tautuatoa*, I explore how the language, progression, and narration of the text show those spaces, relationships and roles motivate certain characters to enter unfamiliar spaces in order to fulfill their needs. I look for actions that show local people moving from familiar local households to unfamiliar spaces in the crowd, and their positive responses to Jesus demonstrate their choosing Jesus's ministry to help them fulfill their needs and roles. Thus, the interactions between Jesus and the crowd are examples of dealing with local needs and roles from the third space of *tautuaileva*.

Fa'asinomaga: Local households

Matt 7:24–29

The phrase ὁμοιωθήσεται ἀνδρὶ φρονίμω, ὅστις ὠκοδόμησεν αὐτοῦ τὴν οἰκίαν ἐπὶ τὴν πέτραν (will be like a wise man who built his house on the rock) provides the setting in which the following healing ministry will be undertaken. The parable is given various labels by scholars, highlighting that the parable is about carrying out actions in connection with households, either literal or metaphorical, of the context that the listeners inhabit. For example, Joachim Jeremias

---

[16] As discussed in the analysis of the character of the crowd in 4:25, the crowd has diverse and ambivalent characteristics. The function of those characteristics in 7:24–8:22 imply that there are various households in the local place of Galilee encoded in the text.

interprets this section as "the parable of the two houses,"[17] while Ulrich Luz calls it "the parable of the builders."[18] The parable is described as building houses: metaphors for those who hear and act upon Jesus's teachings. These households exhibit familiar relationships to which members of the crowd are linked and which determine their roles. This reflects how Jesus's ministry, in this part of the story, is a ministry that considers the needs of local people in relation to their households. Thus, the imagery of house building foreshadows the locality of Jesus's ministry in the following sections.

Matt 8:1–17

The narrator's presentation of Jesus's relationship to the crowd continues into the middle part of the unit. The healing of the leper reveals the first household that Jesus deals with in the unit.[19] The leper belongs to a Jewish household, and so did Jesus. Jesus's belonging to the Jewish household is evident in his sending the leper to go and show himself to the priest.[20] There are various relationships in this healing event that show the locality of the healing activity. First is Jesus's relationship as a Jew to the leper. Second is the leper's relationship to the priest. The leper's role was that of one seeking to become clean.

Second, the healing of the centurion's servant relates to a Gentile household (8:15–13). The centurion and his servants belong to a Roman imperial household.[21] This healing event introduces a different familial relationship: master and servant/slave.

The third household is that of Peter's (8:14–15), the familiar relationship between Peter and his mother-in-law. As well as the sick and those possessed with demons (8:16–17). The narrator's inclusion of these characters suggests that Jesus will deal with each one of the crowd according to her/his situation.

Matt 8:18–22

The story continues on to the other side of the sea, and Matt 8:18–22 is the point of transition to the other side. In this way, 8:18–22 is not only the conclusion of Jesus's ministry to local households on this side of the sea, but also anticipates his proclamation of ἡ βασιλεία τῶν οὐρανῶν on the other side.

---

[17] Joachim Jeremias, *The Parables of Jesus*, NTL (London: SCM Press, 1963), 194.

[18] Luz, *Matthew 1–7*, 386.

[19] In the religious custom of the Jewish people (household) the leper is regarded unclean (Lev 13–14).

[20] This interpretation echoes Jesus as a person from the Davidic line (see Matt 1:1–17). For interpretations of Jesus as Jew in the early chapters of Matthew, see David D. Kupp, *Matthew's Emmanuel: Divine Presence and God's People in the First Gospel*, SNTSMS 90 (Cambridge: Cambridge University Press, 1996), 52–63.

[21] Carter, *Matthew and Empire*, 9–19.

Among the members of the crowd whom Jesus ordered to go over are the scribe and one of Jesus's disciples who represent other local households. The former is from another type of Jewish household and the latter is from a family being tormented by death. Both of these relationships are familiar, and Jesus has several encounters with both households.

The households, relationships, and roles idenified above reveal the connection of Jesus's ministry to the crowd and to local households. This further emphasizes the locality of Jesus's ministry.

Tautuatoa: Local people move into unfamiliar spaces

According to the *tautuaileva* hermeneutic, a sense of identity is determined by a *tautua* entering unfamiliar spaces to find ways to fulfill his/her needs and roles. This is through the lens of *tautuatoa*, through which I explore how the language, progression, and narration of Matt 7:24–8:22 determine the function of the crowd's relationship to Jesus. In particular, it will show the contraction of space from the healing of the leper (in public) to the healing of Peter's mother-in-law (at a local house).

As mentioned earlier, the conjunction οὖν (then) indicates a rhetorical shift in Jesus's preaching from the teachings of ἡ βασιλεία τῶν οὐρανῶν (5:1–7:23) to applying those teachings to the reality that the crowd lived (7:24–29). In this way, οὖν marks the beginning of the next events of Jesus's ministry. Explaining how those events are to be carried out is the purpose of Matt 7:24–29.

Matt 7:24–29

Through the *tautuatoa* lens, the present indicative tense of Jesus's hope for the type of response from the crowd calls attention to the present world encoded in the text: the first century Mediterranean world. Matthew 7:24–27 is Jesus's negotiation of his vision of ἡ βασιλεία τῶν οὐρανῶν in-between the past and future, emphasising the importance of the present time. This negotiation is evident in the narrator's use of past, present, and future to tell Jesus's request to the crowd in 7:24–27.

This is shown, on the one hand, in the word ὁμοιωθήσεται (will be like; in verse 24) in the future indicative passive tense. This verb expresses the eschatological meaning and function of the parable and also indicates the kind of listener Jesus expects. On the other hand, the aorist indicative active tense of the verbs that show the building of the house on the rock and the sand (ᾠκοδόμησεν; v. 24), the coming of the rain and rivers (κατέβη, ἦλθονἦ; v. 25), the blowing of the winds (ἔπενεθσαν, προςέπεσαν; v. 25), and the fall of the house (ἔπεσεν; v. 25), present events that happened in the past. On the other hand, the present indicative tense of the words ἀκούει and ποιεῖ, which describe Jesus's teaching the crowd (7:24) to listen, indicates that now is the time that Jesus wants house building to be undertaken. Such use of these tenses shows that the house built in the past that determines the type of listener in the future is not just an event of the past and a blessing waiting in the future. It is rather a way of life that members of the crowd are to deal with in the present world. Thus, ἀκούει and ποιεῖ show the product of Jesus's negotiation of the proclamation of ἡ βασιλεία τῶν οὐρανῶν in the past and the future, in accordance with the reality of the present world encoded in the text. In other words, ἀκούει and ποιεῖ reveal Jesus's application of the eschatological purpose of his vision of ἡ βασιλεία τῶν οὐρανῶν to the reality of the present world. In this way, Jesus's teaching the crowd can be seen as teaching emerging from his understanding of the function of his vision of ἡ βασιλεία τῶν οὐρανῶν in-between (a third-space) the past, present, and future. Thus, Jesus's teaching the crowd how to listen in the imagery of house building suggests that Jesus assumes that everyone in the crowd is a member of a particular household in the local place of Galilee.

Jesus's teaching for the type of listener he expects is followed by the crowd's astonishment which points to Jesus as the one who has authority. The astonishment of the crowd is followed by Jesus coming down from the mountain with the crowd following him. Jesus's descending is described by the verbal adjective of καταβάντος (having come down) revealing the change of time and of place for what follows. Thus, Jesus's dealing with the needs of the people in the local context of Galilee is in accordance with the reality of life encountered by those people. This evokes two important points that will help the analysis of how Jesus deals with different needs of various crowd members in 7:24–8:22.

First, building and rebuilding the houses/households is to happen now. Second, the wise listeners are to act despite the barriers that may hold them back. In terms of *tautuaileva*, listening and doing are required for moving in-between spaces, from familiar spaces of local households to unfamiliar spaces of the crowd, where one carries out roles linked to one's local household. One thus moves into unfamiliar places without leaving behind one's familiar (household) space. It is where a local person engages in the process of negotiation, choosing which combination of understandings or cultures that might resolve the situation in which s/he is caught. The movement in-between spaces of certain members of the crowd are shown in Jesus's healing activities in the middle part of the unit (8:1–17).

Matt 8:1–17

Matt 8:1–4: Healing the Leper

Jesus's moving down from the mountain is a transition from proclamation (of ἡ βασιλεία τῶν οὐρανῶν with words) to deeds. The conjunction δὲ (but) in 8:1 indicates continuation of the narrative. It also shows the setting of Jesus's healing

activities as a public area where local households are located.[22] The time of healing was at hand (now). The healing of the leper begins with Jesus's
demonstration of the type of listening he preached about.

A *tautua* (servant) is someone in a hierarchy, which determines his/her role.
The *tautua* may have to move out of the familiar spaces s/he is engaged in, such
as family, to unfamiliar spaces, searching for ways to fulfill that role. The leper
is one example. The familiar local space to which the leper belongs is the Jewish
religious household, which defines him as unclean. Through the lens of *tautuatoa*, the leper has a role to play as a member of the Jewish religious community,
and that role is to seek cleansing. The leper's actions make him a servant of the
Jewish religious community.

The leper is the first member of the crowd who responds with action to Jesus's appeal (7:24–27), a movement into in-between spaces. The narrator
introduces the entrance of the leper with the imperative ἰδού (behold) drawing
attention to the fact that something dramatic is going to happen.[23] The interaction between Jesus and the leper shows the leper's movement into unfamiliar
spaces and relationships. Moreover, the use of the conjunction καὶ (and) to con-
nect verse 1 to verse 2 connects the actions undertaken in the two parts.[24] The
leper as a member of the crowd is a sick person unsure of how to make himself
clean. The crowd is from where the leper begins seeking the opportunity he sees
in Jesus to cleanse him. This approach is described by the verbal adjective of
προσελθών (having coming to) which reveals the leper's initiative in going to
Jesus. It is the leper's agency to act according to the time and space in order to
fulfill his need. The leper's kneeling and saying, "Lord if you choose…" expresses the kind of person he was. The leper was seeking in unfamiliar spaces a
way to fulfill his role as a member of the Jewish religious household. In this
way, the leper is outside of his household but he was certainly not outside of the
community. Because he was with the crowd coming down the mountain, the text
suggests that he was a marginal character. This is reflected in the use of the sub-
junctive ἐὰνθέλῃς (if you are willing) in the leper's appeal to Jesus. These words

---

[22] According to Kingsbury, "in healing, Jesus Son of God assumes the role of the servant
of God and ministers to Israel by restoring persons to health or freeing them from their
afflictions" (Kingsbury, *Matthew as Story*, 68).

[23] The leper's healing occurs before Jesus enters Capernaum in 8:5. To Kingsbury, the
placement of this first healing activity is a paradigm that exhibits the purpose of Jesus's
healing activities as a ministry that is aimed at the people of Israel, Matthew's church.
See Jack D. Kingsbury, "The Miracle of the Cleansing of the Leper as an Approach to the
Theology of Matthew," *CurTM* 4.6 (1977): 344–49. For this study, the healing of the
leper is the first example of how a local member of the crowd moves out of the spaces in
which he is recognized, to unfamiliar spaces where there is hope in relation to his need.

[24] Black, *Sentence Conjunctions*, 111–12.

show that the leper saw in Jesus's teaching and authority, help for his impurity. This was why the leper followed Jesus. The result: the leper was healed.

This was not the end of the healing event. Jesus wanted the leper to go and show himself to the priest. The leper is to take advantage of Jesus's ἡ βασιλεία τῶν οὐρανῶν for his re-instatement into the Jewish religious household—Ὅρα μηδενὶ εἴπῃς, ἀλλὰ ὕπαγε σεαυτὸν δεῖξον (See that you say nothing to anyone but go and show yourself). This command exemplifies how a local person should deal with his/her household. First, "not to say a word to anyone"[25] reminds the audience of what Jesus says in his teaching of a good listener in 7:24. That is, words are not enough to show that one has listened. Actions speak louder than words. So the leper being told to go and show himself to the priest without saying a word to anyone is a task undertaken from the space in-between the leper's familiar space of the Jewish religious household and the unfamiliar space of Jesus's vision of ἡ βασιλεία τῶν οὐρανῶν.

Second, the reflexive pronoun σεαυτὸν (yourself) emphasizes the 'type of showing' that Jesus accentuates. That is, the leper has to do it himself and part of this doing is προςένεγκον τὸ δῶρον (offer[ing] the gift or sacrifice).[26] He is to offer service to the Jewish household by giving the gifts required by the purity laws. Thus, acceptance into his religious household depends on the leper's own actions.

Third, the word ὕπαγε meaning depart is an intransitive verb that "always expresses the past tense by the Imperfect."[27] As such, it expresses the 'go' that Jesus commands—and so his healing was the departure point for his returning to the Jewish religious household. In this way, Jesus's expectation of the leper's healing is that he returns to serve his Jewish religious household in light of his experience of ἡ βασιλεία τῶν οὐρανῶν.

Thus, according to *tautuaileva*, the leper's healing and return to the religious household exhibits his reciprocal undertaking of his service roles to his local household and the household of the βασιλεία. Luz's interpretation of the leper's healing does not directly refer to it as a healing in-between spaces but the summation of his interpretation reflects that in-between space understanding: "the healed leper embodies, in a way, the basic unity between discipleship and Israel and is thus a witness for the people."[28]

In this way, the leper is a disciple sent by Jesus to his Jewish religious household, instructed to continue being a Jew according to Jewish customs. From the spatial dimension of "Jesus in a local household" in this rhetorical unit

[25] These words are interpreted by some scholars as showing the messianic secret. See, Hagner, *Matthew 1–13*, 199.
[26] δῶρον as gift is also sacrifice. *BDAG*, s.v. "δῶρον."
[27] Wenham, *The Elements of the New Testament Greek*, 52–54, 103, 203.
[28] Luz, *Matthew 8–20*, 6.

(7:24–8:22), the sending of the leper indicates the beginning of Jesus's entering local houses through those who respond positively to his ministry. Here Jesus instructs the leper to return to his household, and in and through his Jesus's proclamation of ἡ βασιλεία τῶν οὐρανῶν enters the Jewish household.

8:5–13: Healing the Centurion's Servant

The narrator then moves on to show a member of the crowd from a different household, the household of Roman imperial power (8:5–13). Jesus enters Capernaum and is met by the centurion, another character who emerged from the crowd, as did the leper. He was a man with authority who approached Jesus outside in the open space.

The centurion leaves the familiar space of his imperial household to enter the unfamiliar space of the crowd, a space containing people with different purposes in following Jesus. The centurion is another example of a local person seeking help from Jesus at in-between spaces, to fulfill his role as a leader of his household.

The healing narrative of the centurion's servant is controversial. One of the contentious issues is the two designations of the centurion's servants as παῖς (child, in vv. 6 and 8) and δοῦλος (slave, in v. 9, when he explained his authority). The use of δοῦλος is considered straightforward. It implies the hierarchical system that functions in the centurion's household. But the use of παῖς raises questions because παῖς suggests different interpretations of the centurion's relationship to the servant.

One example is that παῖς refers to a domestic slave. This is the position taken by Gundry, for it exhibits a distinction between two types of servants in this healing event. On the one hand, παῖς shows the centurion's sick servant who cannot do any work. And on the other hand, δοῦλος pictures the servant who is not sick and moves about to do the centurion's commands. Gundry implies that παῖς like δοῦλος is a slave.[29] A second example is the interpretation of παῖς as "beloved-son," proposed by Jennings and Liew, who see the term as having sexual connotations, namely, that the παῖς was a male lover of the centurion in a pederastic relationship.[30] For them, there are different functions of παῖς (male lover) and δοῦλος (domestic servant) in this healing event.

These interpretations highlight the difference between παῖς and δοῦλος from the point of view of the servants' relationship to the centurion. For this study, I see παῖς and δοῦλος from the point of view of the centurion as *tautua*. In this

---

[29] Robert H. Gundry, *Matthew: A Commentary on His Literary and Theological Art* (Grand Rapids: Eerdmans, 1982), 142–44; see also France, *The Gospel of Matthew*, 312.
[30] Theodore W. Jennings and Tat-Siong Benny Liew, "Mistaken Identities but Model Faith: Rereading the Centurion, the Chap, and the Christ in Matthew 8:5–13," *JBL* 123 (2004): 467–94.

way, my interpretation leans towards Luz's interpretation of παῖς as son. Luz reads the centurion's relationship to the servant as father-son.[31] For Luz, the centurion was seeking Jesus's help for his servant as "son" not as "slave" (δοῦλος). This entails seeing the servant as someone close to the centurion. As such, παῖς and δοῦλος reveal the kind of leader the centurion was. He was a leader of and a servant to his household. This is evident in these words of the centurion:

> I am a man ... with soldiers under me; and I say to one, "Go," and he goes, and to another, "Come," and he comes, and to my slave, "Do this," and the slave does. (8:9)

Like Jesus who has authority over the sick, the centurion has authority over his soldiers and slaves. However, his reference to his servant as παῖς shows that he cares for the people under his authority. It is an image of a leader who acts as a servant to his household, seen in his diminishing of his status to ensure that help is sought for his servant.

> Lord, I am not worthy to have you come under my roof, but only speak the word, and my servant will be healed. (8:8)

The purpose of this unexpected approach from a Roman leader (and more unusual because it is made to a Jew) is to save a servant. The centurion goes beyond the boundaries of being a Roman leader for the sake of his servant. As a person with recognized status in the Roman imperial household, the centurion could have sent one of his servants to bring Jesus into the house. However, the centurion deals with the situation himself, in the watchful eyes of the crowd. The centurion enters unfamiliar spaces and chooses what he thinks is best for the well-being of his servant.[32] Thus, the narrator's telling of the centurion's approach to Jesus outside in the public space shows the centurion entering the third space (the space to seek help for his servant).

Another moment in this healing event that shows the interaction between Jesus and the centurion as an event dealing with local needs, is the centurion not accepting Jesus's request to come in to his house. This is one of the mystifying

---

[31] Luz, *Matthew 8–20*, 8, 10. Other examples of interpretations that see παῖς as "son" are Hagner, *Matthew 1–13*, 204; Levine, *The Social and Ethnic Dimensions*, 108, 119. Schweizer, *The Good News*, 212.

[32] A Gentile approaching Jesus in such a way on behalf of another person makes the telling and showing of the healing of the centurion's servant similar to the healing of the Canaanite woman (15:21–28). See Wainwright, *Towards a Feminist Critical Reading*, 112–113; David Hill, *The Gospel of Matthew*, NCB (London: Butler & Tanner, 1972), 151; Jennings and Liew, "Mistaken Identities but Model Faith," 469.

aspects of their dialogue. This comes across as inhospitable and disrespectful. For some critics, the reason for the anti-social response of the centurion is implicated in considering Jesus's response in verse 7 as a question. Wainwright's interpretation links it to Jesus's reaction to the Canaanite woman's appeal in 15:23–24. Wainwright regards the pronoun ἐγὼ (I) that begins Jesus's response as indicating a question: "Shall I come and heal him?" For Wainwright, this question makes the centurion enter into a dialogue with Jesus where the centurion speaks of his having authority.[33] Jennings and Liew treat ἐγὼ (I) as indicator of a question as problematic. For them, it makes ἐγὼ (I) in the reply of the centurion a question as well.[34]

However, through *tautuaileva*, seeing the centurion approaching from a third space, Jesus's question is a rhetorical interrogation marker to find out how the centurion as a leader would accept the help he has sought. The centurion's answer admits that he has authority but that will not hold him back from seeking help for his servant. His words reflect a leader who fluctuates in-between being a master and a father figure. It shows the centurion's ability to consider everyone in this healing event to be important.

One of the implications of the centurion's explanation of his authority could be that bringing Jesus (a Jew) into his Roman imperial house would automatically make Jesus part of a household in which the centurion is the person with authority. The centurion is conscious of his role as a Roman leader. Jesus, despite his willingness to enter the centurion's household, respects the situation of the centurion. This is not necessarily to accept the totalizing authority of Roman imperialism, but rather to accept the way the centurion has made his request in terms of Jesus letting him rebuild his own household. The centurion's positive response shows him acting the way he thinks is appropriate in order not only to save his servant but to save his household also.

After Jesus's conversation with the centurion the narrator tells of Jesus's amazement at the centurion.[35] The repetition of λέγω (I say) in verses 9 and 10 indicates the significance of what the centurion has done for his servant. The use of λέγω (I say) as first person in verse 10 states that Jesus is expressing how great the faith of the centurion as intimated by the adverb ἀμὴν (truly). Ἀμὴν

---

[33] Wainwright, *Towards a Feminist Critical Reading*, 113. See also, Warren Carter, *Matthew and the Margins: A Socio-political and Religious*, JSNTSup 204 (Sheffiled: Sheffield Academic, 2000), 201–2.

[34] Jennings and Liew, "Mistaken Identities but Model Faith," 478–79.

[35] Dube's interpretation of this response is that it reveals "the implied author's accommodating stance toward the Roman Empire." Dube, *Postcolonial Feminist Interpretation*, 130–32. From my hermeneutic of *tautuaileva*, Jesus's positive response is an indirect way of dealing with the reality of the situation encountered by the centurion's servant. The implication of Jesus's positive response is that the centurion becomes a means for reaching out to the servants oppressed in the centurion's household.

reveals Jesus's certainty of the centurion's faith. The mention of Israel in this verse provides one reason why the centurion's faith is important, namely, to show reception of Jesus's proclamation of ἡ βασιλεία τῶν οὐρανῶν. This is amplified in verse 11 where λέγω (I say) is used again to emphasize the statement Jesus made in verse 10. Thus the centurion is an example of a person from the crowd with high status who goes beyond hierarchical boundaries to serve someone in need. This is the reason for Jesus's amazement. But Jesus's amazement is not the end of the event.

Like the healing of the leper, the healing of the centurion's servant finishes with Jesus saying to the centurion: Ὕπαγε, ὡς ἐπίστευσας γενηθήτω σοι (Go; let it be done for you according to your faith). In this way, the centurion who enters the unfamiliar spaces of the crowd and of Jesus's vision of ἡ βασιλεία τῶν οὐρανῶν has become familiar with Jesus's proclamation. He returned to familiar space of his imperial household; the centurion, a local person and a member of the crowd, fluctuated in-between spaces. He listened and acted on Jesus's proclamation in order to save his servant.

Because the centurion's response is an example of a member from the crowd who has listened to and acted on Jesus's teachings, Jesus's commanding him to go is the sending of the centurion as a disciple back to his household. The return to his household is not only to witness the healing of his servant but to rebuild his household. Through the centurion, Jesus's proclamation of ἡ βασιλεία τῶν οὐρανῶν enters another local household. In this interpretation, the function of the centurion failing to stop Jesus entering a local household illustrates that the Roman imperial power cannot stop Jesus from attending to local people who are oppressed and colonized. It is important to acknowledge here that the "servant" was not released from oppression and colonization by Jesus. He was left in the imperial household.

8:14–15: Healing Peter's Mother-in-law and Those Possessed with Demons

In the healing of Peter's mother-in-law, Jesus physically took his ministry into a local household. The conjunction καὶ (and) in verse 14 links Jesus's healing ministry to the healing of the centurion's servant.

There is one slight difference between these healing stories. According to Wainwright, the healing of Peter's mother-in-law is unique in that Jesus takes the initiative by approaching the sick person.[36] In terms of *tautuaileva*, I also see this healing event as unique for it demonstrates Jesus's ministry as a place-based ministry in that the local people are linked to the households to which they belong. Jesus takes his ministry into the homes of local people. This shows his courage and agency in entering an unfamiliar space, leaving the space he has been in before in order to help this woman. This entering reveals Jesus's dealing

---

[36] Wainwright, *Towards a Feminist Critical Reading*, 84.

with local needs from in-between spaces. Jesus enters the house, the space of Peter's mother-in-law and, seeing the woman, he heals her.

In the *tautuaileva* reading, the woman's response shows how she deals with her own situation which is in-between spaces. Her first space is the familiar space of Peter's house. It is the space where she lies sick. By Jesus entering her house, she is brought into the unfamiliar space of Jesus's proclamation of ἡ βασιλεία τῶν οὐρανῶν. By touching her hand, Jesus causes the fever to leave her. This is the beginning of her becoming familiar with the space of Jesus's ministry. As such, this mother-in-law enters the third space of Jesus's vision of ἡ βασιλεία τῶν οὐρανῶν. Then "she got up and began to serve Jesus." She responded with actions, and without a word.

This woman's response is an example of a person in need who deals with her situation from where she is in the local society. The imperfect form of the verb διηκόνει shows the beginning of her serving Jesus as well as its continuation, which will take her beyond the boundaries of the patriarchal system that has been holding her in her home. The healing activities that Jesus undertakes are consummated as fulfillment of Isaiah's prophecy of the suffering servant (v. 17). Jesus's healing of this woman and her response present her as a disciple not to the world but to her own household. The conjunction δὲ (but) in verse 16 indicates two different healings: Peter's mother-in-law (vv. 14–15), and those possessed with demons (v. 16). The focus is on Peter's mother-in-law with a reference to verse 16 to show the time of day the healing ministry ends. As the last healings of the day, they point readers to Matthew's use of Isaiah's prophecy in verse 17 to assert the authority of Jesus the healer as servant of God.[37]

The healing of Peter's mother-in-law is also important in the sense that it reveals the culmination of the development of Jesus's ministry in this unit, namely to take the proclamation of ἡ βασιλεία τῶν οὐρανῶ into local houses and families. From the Roman imperial household of the centurion, Jesus enters a local house to heal Peter's mother-in-law. Even the boundaries which could have held Jesus back did not prevent him from entering.[38]

---

[37] France, *The Gospel of Matthew*, 321. France speaks of that point as "this brief traditional summary [verse 16] is ... made to serve a special purpose as the introduction for a formula-quotation which draws out the significance of this aspect of Jesus's ministry." France treats the healing of Peter's mother-in-law separately from verses 16–17.

[38] See Elaine M. Wainwright's interpretation of this healing as the Matthean re-telling of Mark's source in *Women Healing*, 143–44. Wainwright sees the Matthean re-telling of the healing of Peter's mother-in-law as a "borderland story."

Matt 8:18–22[39]

Considering the healing activities in 8:1–17 as works carried out in one day, I can imagine the purpose of the narrator in 8:18–22, which foreshadows a shift from one side of the sea to another.

Matt 8:18–22 is considered a very important passage in defining the nature of discipleship. Common interpretations include, first, that the scribe is a disciple of Jesus.[40] Second, Jesus's response to the scribe shows the protagonist's homelessness as well as the difficulty of discipleship.[41] One's obligations, such as one's responsibility to one's family, are considered secondary to Jesus's min-

---

[39] Matt 8:18–22 has been interpreted as exhibiting the cost of becoming a disciple. That is, a disciple should abandon his family and follow Jesus. Luz's interpretation from the ecclesiological point of view suggests that "this harsh saying of Jesus (*Follow me and let the dead bury their own dead*) was not intended to give general instructions about how people should act any more than the demand to give up everything and to follow Jesus was a requirement for everybody" (Luz, *Matthew 8–20*, 19–20. Luz's interpretation accentuates the consequence of following, which is leaving the family. Undertaking discipleship is not an easy decision to make. It requires the sacrifice of things that are dear to the disciple. See also Jack D. Kingsbury, "On Following Jesus: The 'Eager' Scribe and the 'Reluctant' Disciple (Matthew 8:18–22)," *NTS* 34 (1988): 45–59. Kingsbury, *Matthew as Story*, 134; John Nolland, *The Gospel of Matthew*, NIGTC (Grand Rapids: Eerdmans, 2005), 368–69; Ulrich Luz, *Matthew 8–20* (Minneapolis: Fortress, 2001), 18–20, France, *The Gospel of Matthew*, 328–31.

Hengel emphasises the function of Jesus as Messiah in calling disciples to follow. According to Hengel, Jesus's calling shows Jesus a Messiah who proclaims the kingdom of God (Hengel, *The Charismatic Leader*, 69). Despite this difference between Hengel's and Luz's interpretations, they both consider that leaving home is not easy. Reflected in their interpretations is the view that discipleship is a mission that needs to be built and spread to the global level. Luz's and Hengel's interpretations view discipleship in the master-disciple relationship. Those traditional interpretations overlook the disciple's connection to family (8:22).

[40] See Hagner, *Matthew 1–13*, 217; Schweizer, *The Good News*, 218–20; Hill, *The Gospel of Matthew*, 161–62. These interpretations are based on the interpretation of εἷς (one) in verse 19 and ἕτερος (another) in verse 21, and on the consideration of scribe in other parts of the story as followers of Jesus—13:52, 23:34.

Some scholars however disagree, including Kingsbury ("On Following Jesus," 48) who argued that εἷς is also used in Matthew as the indefinite article so that the scribe in verse 19 can be referred to as a "scribe." Thus, Kingsbury argues that the scribe is not a called disciple of Jesus but a would-be disciple. See also, Kingsbury, "The Verb *AKOLOUTHEIN*," 58–61.

[41] For example, according to Moxnes, Jesus's response to the scribe presents "'the son of man' as a wanderer who 'does not have anywhere to lay his head'… This is a picture of a man without a house and shelter; we might say a vagabond or a homeless person." Moxnes, *Putting Jesus in His Place*, 49–50.

istry. The dominant interpretation of this text is that it is about the cost of being a disciple.[42] This traditional interpretation continues to "hold court." However, abandoning one's obligations to family is not all there is to the narration and progress of the text. Through the lens of *tautuatoa*, Matt 8:18–22 presents discipleship as giving attention to the needs and rights of local people.

After the appropriation of an Isaian prophecy re-affirming Jesus's authority and role as servant of God, the narrative unit comes to an end. "Going over to the other side" both points to the ending of the unit and also anticipates the continuation of Jesus's relationship to the crowd in the next part of the story. Verses 18–22 is a kind of hiatus because there is no going over to the other side of the sea until verse 23. In terms of *tautuaileva*, verses 18–22 anticipates the transition from one side of the sea to the other. In this way, as I mentioned above, it cuts across the traditional consideration of verses 23–34 as part of 8:18–22.

My consideration of 8:18–22 as the ending part of the unit begins from the words Ἰδὼνδὲ (and having seen) in verse 18. The conjunction δὲ links 8:18–22 to the previous healing events and Ἰδὼν as a verbal adjective is a description of how Jesus saw the crowd that came to him in verse 16. The crowd was made up of many sick people possessed with demons. The time these people came to Jesus was *evening*. Thus, verse 16 offers one of the reasons why Jesus ordered the crowd to go over the other side: it was near darkness. This reason is important to the analysis of Jesus's dialogue with the scribe (vv. 19–20) and the disciple (vv. 21–22), which is again emphasized by the conjunction δὲ. The ending is thus linked to the healings in 8:1–17 to reveal a different set of events: first, Jesus tells the crowd to go over to the other side; second, a scribe approaches Jesus; third, another of Jesus's disciples makes a request to Jesus. Through the lens of *tautuatoa*, these events assert the type of listening that Jesus has taught and practised since 7:24–8:17 as the way to fulfill the needs of local people.

---

[42] Hengel interprets Jesus calling the disciple in 8:21 to follow him as a contrast to the scribe asking to follow Jesus in 8:19–20. To Hengel, the kind of discipleship Matthew emphasises is not a rabbinical teacher-pupil type of relationship but eschatological as exhibited in Jesus's answer to let the dead bury their own dead (8:22). Hengel, *The Charismatic Leader*, 14–15, 69.

Kingsbury interprets the scribe as "eager" and the disciple as "reluctant." He considers the scribe's appeal (in accordance with Jesus's reply) negative, and the disciple's request positive. The disciple shows commitment to discipleship more important than one's obligations. See Kingsbury, "On Following Jesus," 45–49. This type of commitment is also affirmed in Theissen's and Edwards' interpretations. Theissen regards Matt 8:20 as anticipation of the type of mission that will be carried out by the twelve in 10:1–45. According to Theissen, the twelve are wandering charismatics who will be homeless (Theissen, *The First Followers of Jesus*, 10–14); and for Edwards it was "absolute, immediate commitment" (Edwards, *Matthew's Narrative Portrait of Disciples*, 30).

After Jesus orders the crowd to go over to the other side of the sea (in verse 23), a scribe emerges from the crowd, approaches Jesus and asks to follow him. This character is one of those that Jesus teaches to become the listeners of his ministry. The narrator's inclusion of the scribe and disciple as two different characters reveals the kind of following Jesus wants from those he summoned in this part of his ministry.

One of the contentious issues in the dialogue between Jesus and the scribe is whether or not the scribe is a disciple.[43] Scribes were historically members of the Jewish leaders' circle and so interpretations that focus on this aspect tend to see the scribe's request in a negative light. In Kingsbury's interpretation, Jesus's response adds to the irony of considering the scribe as a disciple. However, considering the scribe as a member of the crowd makes his request to follow not a surprising one. This scribe is different from other Jewish leaders, and his identity is ambiguous as indicated by the adjective εἷς (one) used to identify him as "one scribe" or "a scribe." The scribe's request at the end of the unit reveals that he understood Jesus's vision of ἡ βασιλεία τῶν οὐρανῶν.

After the scribe listened to and witnessed Jesus's teaching and healing activities, he addressed Jesus as "teacher." He respected Jesus and his teachings. The statement ἀκολουθήσς σοι ὅπου ἐὰν ἀπερχῃ (I will follow you wherever you might go) is in the future tense and expresses a promise. The future tense implies that the scribe was already a follower.[44] His appeal reveals his willingness to go with Jesus wherever Jesus decides. The scribe was a disciple of Jesus.

That the scribe was a disciple is also reflected in Jesus's positive response. This reading takes into account that it was "evening" (8:16), the end of a long day of healing activities (8:1–17). It has been a long day of work, and so responses to the scribe: "Foxes have holes, and birds of the air have nests; but the Son of Man has nowhere to lay his head." There is irony in this response. One interpretation considers this response to reveal the scribe's request as negative in the sense that the scribe's motive was the same as other Jewish leaders for following Jesus's ministry—they followed to find a way to denounce Jesus and his ministry. However, there is nothing in this response that shows Jesus looking at this scribe's request as such. This response could be alerting the scribe to the next part of the ministry which will be carried out through the night. Jesus's response does not counter the scribe's request but rather indicates how the ministry will continue. Despite Jesus's willingness to continue his ministry, he did

---

[43] See Kingsbury, "On Following Jesus," 45–59; Robert H. Gundry, "On True and False Disciples in Matthew 8.18–22," *NTS* 40.3 (1994): 433–41.

[44] Gundry's interpretation reflects this claim by considering the word "followed" in 8:23 as an implication of the following in 8:19 and 22 to be carried out by those who are already disciples of Jesus such as those in 4:20 and 22. Gundry, "On True and False Disciples," 437.

not want his followers blind to the danger they will face. While foxes and birds have places to go when there is danger, the Son of Man, in fulfilling his mission, has nowhere to hide from danger. If the scribe as Jewish leader follows Jesus, he would be in danger in the eyes of the Jewish religious household.

I see Jesus's response to the scribe as showing that discipleship was a restless mission. This is pictured in the phrase οὐκ ἔχει ποῦ τὴν κεφαλὴν κλίνῃ (has nowhere he might lay the head). The word κλίνη means "to cause something to incline or bend" or "to sleep" and plays an important part in the phrase. It has the sense of "voluntary act"[45] and is the word used to describe the bowing of Jesus's head before he died in John 19:30. Thus, "lay the head" gives the impression that discipleship is like voluntary death; "lay the head" is ministry without rest.

After the scribe's request, another disciple of Jesus approached him. He wanted to go and bury his father. The adjective Ἕτερος (another) in verse 21 suggests that the scribe is another disciple. The requests of the two disciples are pointed out with the conjunction δὲ (but another): the first disciple (the scribe) asks to follow, the other asks to return to his family. Jesus did not deny the local customs of the people. What is important is that one should deal with the needs of the people in their situation.

The second disciple was a family person who knew his role as a son. He is obligated to go and bury his father. This dialogue has been interpreted as showing that family was to be abandoned when one becomes a disciple. It appears as if Jesus placed more value on following him than on commitment to family. Would a son leave his dead father without saying good bye? This son should not consider himself part of the family he has left behind. Was this what Jesus wanted?

Through the lens of *tautuaileva*, this is not the only way that the text may be interpreted. The disciple speaks to Jesus in the evening. That was not the time of the day to bury a family member. Later in the story (9:1), Jesus is shown getting into the boat and returning to Capernaum. The disciple who requested to go and bury his father would have been part of Jesus'scompany returning to Capernaum. As such, Jesus's saying "Follow me and let the dead bury the dead" washis telling the disciple to follow because night time is not a good time to bury his father. When they returned to Capernaum the next day, that would be the appropriate time for the disciple to go and bury his father. Thus, Jesus's response to the disciple is not a command to abandon his obligation to his family but to wait until the appropriate time.

---

[45] *BDAG*, s.v. "Κλίνω."

Summary

Jesus's relationship to the crowd in this unit deals with the needs that were pertinent to the local place of Galilee. First, I have shown through the lens of *fa'asinomaga* that certain members of the crowd belonged to local households (familiar spaces). Those households determined their roles. Second, identifying those households, relationships, and roles through a *tautuaileva* reading demonstrated those crowd members' positive responses to Jesus's ministry. They go beyond familiar local household spaces to enter the less familiar spaces of the crowd, and the space of Jesus's proclamation of ἡ βασιλεία τῶν οὐρανῶν, in order to find ways that fulfill their needs and roles. Such movements made them approach Jesus from in-between or third spaces.

This analysis has shown that 7:24–8:22 reveals an important characteristic of becoming a disciple, namely, that Jesus summoned members of the crowd to listen, and those who listened were sent back to help their households. Listening to Jesus's proclamation involves entering a third space where one deals with local needs in light of the situations in which those in need are caught. As such, there are other disciples apart from the twelve. The following inter-textual and social and cultural textual analyses will elaborate on this reading.

Inter-textures: Isa 53:4

This section analyses Matthew's recitation of Isa 53:4 to show how attending to the needs of local people in Matt 7:24–8:22 requires courage and endurance. Moreover, it will underscore the difficulty of discipleship as a local mission.

I first explore how the Matthean recitation of Isa 53:4a functions in the progress of 7:24–8:22 as a rhetorical unit. The Matthean recitation is linked to Jesus's preaching, teaching, and healing in Matthew chapters 5 to 8.[46] The second part of this analysis explores the Matthean reconfiguration of Isa 53:4a. One of the dominant interpretations of this prophecy is that it announces the

---

[46] Because 7:24–29 as the conclusion of the Sermon on the Mount is considered the beginning part of 7:24–8:22 as a rhetorical unit, therefore, Matthew's recitation of Isa 53:4a in Matt 8:17 is considered to relate also to the Sermon on the Mount. This interpretation is also based on considering the day that culminates in the mention of 'evening' in 8:16 to have begun from Matt 5:1. I will explain later how this analysis considered 5:1–8:17 as one whole day of work in Matthew's presentation of Jesus's ministry. This does not make the analysis refer to the whole Sermon on the Mount. As mentioned in the rhetorical and narrative analysis of 7:24–8:22 as a rhetorical unit, 7:24–29 as Jesus's announcing of the kind of listener expected in his vision of ἡ βασιλεία τῶν οὐρανῶν is interpreted as the beginning of Jesus's uttering of the application of the Sermon. Thus, this analysis' referring to Matt 5 to 7 is actually a reference to 7:24–29 as representation of the Sermon in light of the context of 7:24–8:22 emphasised in this study.

vicarious and redemptive suffering of God's servant.[47] The servant is revealed to take upon himself the suffering of God's people. In the following analysis, the Matthean reconfiguration show that the servant's taking of other people's suffering does not mean that s/he carries upon himself or herself the suffering of others but that s/he helps others carry their own suffering.

The following questions guide the analysis. How does Matthew's recitation and recontextualization of Isa 53:4a reveal the type of servant that Jesus portrays in 7:24–8:22? How does that type of servanthood intertextually show Jesus's sense of belonging to Galilee? How does the social and cultural nature of 7:24–8:22 show Jesus's taking of his ministry to local households as honoring their members? How does the text depict the positive responses of members of the crowd as responses of honor? How does the narrator show these interactions as reflecting Jesus's attention to the needs and rights of local people in accordance with their situations in the local place of Galilee?

Recitation of Isa 53:4a

The Matthean narrator recites Isa 53:4a in 8:17.[48] The narrator attributes the prophecy to Isaiah and claims its fulfillment in the healing actions of Jesus in 8:1–16.[49] The attribution draws the reader's attention to Isaiah as a prophet, in order to help them understand Jesus's undertaking of the healing activities and their purposes. The recitation affirms the functions of Jesus's character as healer and the sick members of the crowd as the sufferers. It alerts readers that Jesus here puts into actions his vision of ἡ βασιλεία τῶν οὐρανῶν.

---

[47] See John N. Oswalt, *The Book of Isaiah Chapters 40–66*, NICOT (Grand Rapids: Eerdmans, 1998), 375–408; John D. W. Watts, *Isaiah 34–66*, WBC (Texas: Word Books, 1987), 222–33; Brevard S. Childs, *Isaiah*, OTL (Louisville: Westminster John Knox, 2001), 407–23.

[48] See Hagner, *Matthew 1–13*, 210; Hill, *The Gospel of Matthew*, 160–61.

[49] Some scholars interpreted Matthew's recitation of Isa 53 as showing the vicarious suffering of the servant (e.g., Keener, *The Gospel of Matthew*, 273; W. D. Davies and Dale C. Allison, *A Critical and Exegetical Commentary on the Gospel according to Saint Matthew VIII–XVIII*, 38). For others, it is about the healing activities (e.g., Hill, *The Gospel of Matthew*, 160–61; Wainwright, *Towards a Feminist Reading*, 82; Luz, *Matthew 8–10*, 14. Novakovic, "Matthew's Atomistic Use of the Scripture," 147–62).

The healing in chapters 8 and 9 have been read as 'miracles' (Hagner, *Matthew 1–13*, 210; Schweizer, *The Good News*, 217) which disguises the healing activities themselves (Elaine M. Wainwright, "The Matthean Jesus and the Healing of Women," in *The Gospel of Matthew in Current Study*, ed. David E. Aune [Grand Rapids: Eerdmans, 2001], 74–95). It is argued in this analysis that Jesus's carrying of the suffering of others is not about redemptive suffering but actual dealing with the needs of the local people as a long day of work. This is no miracle.

The arrangement of the rhetorical unit indicates how the recitation functions in the progression of the narration of Jesus's ministry. The recitation (8:17) is in the middle section of the unit (8:1–17), and reflects the narrator's summary of Jesus's putting into action his vision of ἡ βασιλεία τῶν οὐρανῶν. As mentioned in the innertextual analysis above, 7:24–29 is the conclusion of Jesus's Sermon on the Mount, and the beginning of the application of Jesus's teaching and preaching of the obligations of the βασιλεία, which could be seen in Jesus's interaction with the crowd in 8:1–16. These include the healings of the leper, the centurion's servant, Peter's mother-in-law,[50] and the sick and those possessed by demons. Because the narrator's recitation of Isa 53:4a is interpreted as a summary of Jesus's actions made before 8:17, the recitation also reasserts the significance of those actions.

Reconfiguration of Isa 53:4a[51]

I analyse the reconfiguration of the Masoretic and LXX texts. The small changes that Matthew makes have intertextual ramifications in clarifying the significance of the Matthean presentation of the locality of Jesus's ministry in Galilee. My analysis is concerned with the reconfigured text which echoes and mimics the suffering servant in the Isaiah literary context. The three versions of Isa 53:4a are:

LXX (Isa 53:4a)
οὗτος τὰς ἁμαρτίας ἡμῶν φέρει καὶ περὶ ἡμῶν ὀδυνᾶται
He bears our sins and is pained for us

MT (Isa 53:4a)
אכן חלינו הוא נשא ומכאבינו סבלם
Surely he has borne our infirmities and carried our diseases

---

[50] According to Wainwright, the healing of Peter's mother-in-law is the "climatic point" of the first three healing stories, linked to the "motif of Jesus' liberating activity" in the fulfillment quotation of verses 16–17. That link has close connection to verses 18–22 which accentuates the liberating motif. Wainwright points to a connection of the healing activities in 8:1–17 to 8:18–22 but she did not elaborate on it. The analysis presented here offers an elaboration: liberating the suffering of others is not easy. It is indeed very hard work.

[51] Maarten Menken suggests that Matthew worked from a revised LXX text. See Maarten J. J. Menken, "The Source of the Quotation from Isaiah 53:4 in Matthew 8:17," *NovT* 39.4 (1997), 313–27. For another textual analysis of Matthew's recitation of Isa 53:4, see, Novakovic, "Matthew's Atomistic Use of the Scripture," 147–62.

Matt 8:17

Αὐτὸς τὰς ἀσθενείας ἡμῶν ἔλαβεν καὶ τὰς νόσους ἐβάστασεν
He took our infirmities and bore our diseases

There are similarities between the three texts. The Matthean text mimics the MT and LXX through a rendering of the subject of the prophecy in the third person. The subject (the servant) is a person of importance. The MT identifies the subject with the third person masculine pronoun הוא. He is revealed after אכן (surely) which expresses assertiveness. The Matthean use of αὐτὸς (he) echoes that emphasis. The personal pronoun αὐτὸς implicitly expresses the subject as "he himself." Despite the Matthean recitation not given an explicit translation of אכן (surely), its use of αὐτὸς mimics this element. The assertive sense presents the importance of the subject—the "servant", and his/her task of carrying other people's suffering. In 7:24–8:22, that subject is identified as Jesus who proclaims the good news and puts it into action. Jesus playing the role of teacher, preacher, and healer of ἡ βασιλεία τῶν οὐρανῶν makes him the Servant of God in the present world encoded in the text.

Second, the Matthean text echoes the MT's rendering of the prophecy as an action completed in the past. The MT uses the verbs נשא and סבלם (he has borne and carried) in their perfect tense expressing an action that is complete. In the context of Isa 53 in the MT, that perfect tense reveals that the God-given servant has already set foot on earth (Isa 52:7) and has taken upon himself the suffering of God's people. Who that servant is in Isa 53 is not unclear.

The Matthean recitation encodes traces of the Isaiah text's reference to Israel's return from exile in Babylon. It was the time when the Persian Empire led by Cyrus displaced the Assyrian Empire.[52] According to that background, some scholars identified the servant as Israel. Others identified the servant as Cyrus, and some saw the servant as a prophet himself. At this stage of my *tautuaileva* reading, it is not important who the servant is in Isa 53:4. What is important here is that the servant has already arrived. This aspect is reflected in the Matthean reconfiguration of Isa 53:4a, in the use of the verbs ἔλαβεν (he took) and ἐβάστασεν (he bore). These verbs in their aorist tense express the complete sense of the prophecy. The narrative placement of the recitation after the healing actions of Jesus in 8:1–16 suggests that the taking of infirmities and diseases was already done by Jesus in 7:24–8:16.

---

[52] See, Walter Brueggemann, *Isaiah 40–66*, NICOT (Louisville: Westminster John Knox, 1998), 1–2; Watts, *Isaiah 34–66*, 227–29; Oswalt, *The Book of Isaiah Chapters 40–66*, 7–10.

The Matthean recitation carries the Masoretic meaning of הלינו in the word ἀσθενείας (sickness).[53] This is the only Matthean use of the word ἀσθενείας and the suffering that Jesus is dealing with here is physical sickness. Thus, the Matthean rendering of הלינו as ἀσθενείας suggests that the sickness is the weakening of bodily strength. The verbs ἔλαβεν and ἐβάστασεν show a type of taking and carrying of people's suffering that differs from the MT and LXX. The word ἔλαβεν comes from λαμβάνω and is translated as "he or she took away or removed." The Matthean use of ἐβάστασεν shows another alteration which affirms the narrator's link to the immediate context of Jesus's preaching, teaching, and healing ministry.[54]

In the second part of the prophecy, the MT and LXX texts speak of the servant bearing of other people's diseases and sins and is pictured in ומכאבינו סבלם (to carry or bear our diseases) and 'καὶ περὶ ἡμῶν ὀδυνᾶται' (and concerning our having pain) as part of the vicarious suffering mentioned in the first part of the sentence (אכן הלינו הוא נשא—Surely, he has borne our infirmities; οὗτος τὰς ἁμαρτίας ἡμῶν φέρει—This man bears our sins). For the Matthean recitation, ἐβάστασεν diverts from the sense in the MT and LXX. The Matthean text is not about carrying diseases upon himself but draws attention to the endurance of the long day of work (toward "evening" in Matt 8:16). This reading is based on the Matthean use of the verb βαστάζω (sustain a burden) in relation to a long day of work. The first Matthean use of the verb βαστάσαι is in 3:11, in the aorist infinitive active to describe John the Baptist's admitting that he is not fit to carry Jesus's sandals. The context in which John the Baptist proclaimed ἡ βασιλεία τῶν οὐρανῶν is the wilderness of Judea (3:1). That was where John the Baptist wore clothing of camel's hair, and ate locusts and wild honey (3:4). Working in that environment was not easy, and the narrator's use of Βαστάσαι strengthens a link between John's words (he is not fit enough to carry Jesus's sandals) and John's long days of working in the heat of the wilderness (3:1–4). Thus, John the Baptist's words (3:11) are not about humbleness but not having physical strength and energy to carry on the proclamation of ἡ βασιλεία τῶν οὐρανῶν.

Another use of βαστάζω is its aorist participle active (Βαστάσασι—having borne) that describes the actions of the labourer who have worked all day long in

---

[53] According to Martin Hengel, the LXX's rendering of Isa 53 strengthens vicarious suffering emphasis which is lacking in the Jewish sources. Martin Hengel, "The Effective History of Isaiah 53 in the Pre-Christian Period," in *The Suffering Servant: Isaiah 53 in Jewish and Christian Sources*, ed. Bernd Janowski and Peter Stuhlmacher (Grand Rapids: Eerdmans, 2004), 119. See also David Hill, "Son and Servant," 9.

[54] Two interpretations help clarify my interpretation of ἐβάστασεν. Menken spoke of Matthew's use of ἐβάστασεν as stressing the idea of "taking away" and he linked that to βαστάζω in Matt 3:11 and 20:12 (Menken, "The Source of the Quotation from Isaiah 53:4," 322). Novakovic also interpreted it to have embodied the idea of 'the carrying away' as in ἔλαβεν (Novakovic, "Matthew's Atomistic Use of the Scripture," 156).

the heat in the parable of the labourers in the vineyard in 20:11. This use of βαστάζω is linked to "evening," the time of the day in which the owner of the vineyard calls the labourers and gives them their pay (20:8). The Matthean recitation of Isa 53:4a also exhibits that link of "carrying" to a "long day of work." The use of ἐβάτασεν in 8:17 is a rendering of סבל (to bear or carry). Its function in the Matthean recitation links to "evening" in verse 16, the time of the day that culminates the long day of work Jesus faced which began with preaching on the mountain (7:24–29) and continued to healing activities (8:1–16). Some critics do not consider "evening" important in defining the meaning and purpose of Jesus's healing actions.[55] I consider "evening" important especially in its connection to ἐβάστασεν. The connection pictures the kind of suffering Matthew speaks about in this part of the story. The Matthean intertextual reciting of Isa 53:4a bears the meaning of carrying another person's suffering but not in the sense of vicarious suffering. Rather, it expresses the endurance of the long day of work that Jesus encountered by helping those in need.[56] Thus, carrying away other people's suffering in and through a long day of work is significant in the whole unit (7:24–8:22). It closes the middle section of the unit, anticipating the reasons for Jesus's responses to the scribe and to one of his disciples (8:18–22). It anticipates that Jesus's response to the scribe is not about not having a home or house. Rather, carrying away the suffering of local people is not easy. It is a restless mission. It takes time and energy.

The Matthean use of ἐβάστασεν has connection to τάς νόσους (diseases). Matthew uses νόσος five times to characterise the task of taking away diseases as a heavy burden. The use in Matt 4:23 and 24 are connected to Jesus's going throughout Galilee. The use in Matt 9:35 and 10:1 links to Jesus's going throughout the cities and villages. Their connections to "going throughout" (in the imperfect tense) show Matthew's use of νόσος as an assertion that taking away people's diseases was not an easy mission. Jesus's healings completed in 8:1–16 is hard work undertaken throughout the whole day. Matthew's reconfiguration foreshadows how the continuation of that task will be undertaken in the next part of the ministry.

---

[55] For example, France writes that the time of the day mentioned in Mark is important as it reveals the day Jesus healed the sick in Peter's mother-in-law's house. Because a day is not mentioned in Matthew, France sees "evening" in verse 16 as having little significance to the meaning of the sentence. For France, the focus of verse 16 was to anticipate the uttering of the fulfillment quotation in verse 17 whose central emphasis is the authority of Jesus as healer (France, *The Gospel of Matthew*, 321). In my *tautuaileva* reading, what is important is the time of the day.

[56] According to Schweizer, the reason why Matthew omitted the Sabbath as the day of the healings mentioned in Mark is because it was no longer Sabbath (Schweizer, *The Good News*, 217).

Summary

Matthew's recitation and reconfiguration of Isa 53:4a is affirmation of Jesus's actions in 7:24–8:22 pertinent to the needs of the local people in the world encoded in the text. It affirms other characteristics of discipleship emphasised in this study, giving primary attention to local needs of local households. The analysis revealed that Matthew's recitation of Isa 53:4a relates to the progress of Jesus's healing actions. Jesus's undertaking of the servant's role is to carry the suffering of those in need, an undertaking made from in-between spaces. Despite Jesus being the Son of God and Messiah, his actions in Matt 7:24–8:22 as teacher, preacher and healer make him a servant who deals with the suffering of others according to the reality of their world. The healed as family members are disciples that Jesus sends back to their households to serve their families. The analysis of the Matthean reconfiguration of the recitation of Isa 53:4a elaborated on that function. It demonstrated that the reconfiguration expressed and pictured Matthew's emphasis on the servant's taking away the suffering of others, rather than the servant's taking the people's suffering upon himself or herself.

Jesus gave the crowd members the opportunity to play their part in maintaining and continuing to fulfill their needs. Thus, the Matthean recitation of Isa 53:4a was made in accordance with the inclusive nature of Jesus's vision of ἡ βασιλεία τῶν οὐρανῶν. In this way, the intertextural analysis has affirmed that Jesus's relationship to the crowd in Matt 7:24–8:22 reveals other important characteristics of becoming a disciple. Becoming a disciple means helping to take away the sufferings of others. Moreover, a disciple is to return to help take away the sufferings encountered by his/her own family, household, and group members.

Social and Cultural Textures: Honor and Shame

The aim of the analysis of the social and cultural textures of the text is to explore how the first century Mediterranean social and cultural value of honor and shame, and Jesus's reversal of that value, are encoded in Matt 7:24–8:22. In this analysis, firstly, through the lens of *fa'asinomaga*, I identify the local household systems encoded in the text as reflected in the characters of certain members of the crowd in the story. These systems are hierarchical and patriarchal; part of identifying those encoded households is to show who were considered as honorable and who were regarded as shameful. Secondly, I explore the social and cultural textures of the text as rhetoric of praise and blame revealing Jesus's calling the crowd to listen, for the sake/honor of ἡ βασιλεία τῶν οὐρανῶν. This reveals members of the crowd who leave the spaces of their household and enter unfamiliar spaces, and who face challenges against the fulfilling of their needs and their roles as members of households. Their positive responses to Jesus's ministry will be interpreted as outcomes of entering in-between spaces.

Honor and Shame

The world encoded in the text is the local place of Galilee in the first century Mediterranean world. The literary role and function of certain characters as members of the crowd reflect the local household systems in the first century Mediterranean world. The first household system is displayed in relation to the leper who is from a Jewish religious household system (8:1–4). The aspect of the Jewish religious belief that linked the leper to his Jewish household is its purity codes. Purity in the Jewish system defines the boundaries that separate those who obey the law, seen as clean, from those who are outside the system, seen as unclean and therefore sinners (Lev 13:1–14:57).[57] This system empha-sizes cleanliness and uncleanliness in Jews' relationship to God, and to each other. The elders and priests are at the top level of the hierarchy of this system; the leper as the unclean one is at the lowest level of this hierarchy. He was an outcast.

The leper can become clean if s/he is declared clean by the priest after going through the ritual of cleansing (Lev 14:1–57). In Matthew's text the narrator often speaks of the Jewish community in regard to their synagogues (e.g., Matt 6:2, 5; 12:9) and their conflicts with Jesus's ministry. Whether there were syna-gogues in the time of Jesus's ministry in Galilee is debated. Archaeological studies dated the excavated synagogues in the Galilee to several years later than the first century.[58] However, in considering the importance of the literary con-struction of the text, Horsley sees the synagogue not as a building but an assembly or community of local people.[59] Thus, Moxnes argues that "in Galilee at the time of Jesus, synagogues most likely were gathering places for the vil-lage, covering broad range of communal affairs and dominated by local community leaders."[60] The leper would have belonged to such a"synagogue"— acommunity of local Jewish people. This community is led by elders and priests who implement strict purity lawsin and through religious rituals and practices. So Jesus's healing of the leper helps reinstate him into his Jewish (household) community.

The next household is the Roman imperial household, in the story of the centurion and his servants (8:5–13). In the first century Mediterranean world,

---

[57] See Ched Myers, *Binding the Strong Man: A Political Reading of Mark's Story of Je-sus* (Maryknoll: Orbis, 1988), 75–77; Bruce J. Malina, *The New Testament World: Insights from Cultural Anthropology* (Minneapolis: Fortress, 1993), 149–83.

[58] See Eric M. Meyers, "Ancient Synagogues: An Archaeological Introduction," in *Sa-cred Realm: The Emergence of the Synagogue in the Ancient World*, ed. Steven Fine (Oxford: Oxford University Press, 1996), 3–20.

[59] Horsley, *Archaeology, History and Society in Galilee*, 7–8, 132–55.

[60] Halvor Moxnes, *Putting Jesus in His Place*, 152–53.

the Roman imperial system was headed by the emperor as the paterfamilias.[61] Next to the emperor was a small group of ruling elites made up of highly regarded officials (such as military and religious leaders) chosen by the emperor. These officials were the governing class chosen to represent the emperor in the cities and countries ruled by the Roman Empire. According to Carter, the Roman imperial system was controlled by two percent of the population and was made up with people of recognized status and enforced by the might of Roman military power.[62] Some of the wealth from lands and productions earned by the Roman Empire through taxation and loan schemes were shared by members of this group. The group next to (below) the governing officials was the retainers who assisted the governing class in the cities. The people in this group also received some rewards for their work but far less than what was received by the governing officials. The last group in the system was the rest of the population including peasants and artisans. The centurion as a military leader is part of the governing class appointed to the area of Galilee. Thus, in the Roman imperial system, the emperor and his official and retainers are examples of people who have honor. This would include the household of the centurion.

The next household in the text is that of Peter. According to the social and cultural context of the first century Mediterranean world, local family and kinship households were ran and controlled by the paterfamilias system. The father was the head of the family and every other member of the family were his children. The narrator speaks of the house Jesus enters in 8:14–15 as the house of Peter, implying that Peter was the father or head of this household.

Other households in the text include the households of the sick and those possessed by demons. The sicknesses of the πολλούς in verse 16 is part of the Galilean community that needs help. The households associated with the scribe (8:19–20) and one of Jesus's disciples (8:21–22) are no different from the households I described above. The scribe as a Jewish leader belongs to the Jewish religious household. Jesus's disciple who asked to go and bury his father belongs to the type of household to which Peter's mother-in-law belonged that is, a household that is controlled by the paterfamilias.

It is apparent who in these households are in the place of honor and who in the place of shame. The father as the head of the family is the person with honor, and the rest, such as women, have the status of shame. However, Jesus's proclamation of ἡ βασιλεία τῶν οὐρανῶν in 7:24–8:22 reverses that structure into his

---

[61] Stephan F. Joubert, "Managing the Household: Paul as *Paterfamilias* of the Christian Household Group in Corinth," in *Modelling Early Christianity: Social-scientific Studies of the New Testament in Its Context*, ed. Philip F. Esler (New York: Routledge, 1995), 213–15.

[62] Carter, *Matthew and Empire*, 9–17.

vision according to which everyone is honorable regardless of status and gender if s/he listens and acts upon his teaching.

Jesus's Reversal of the Honor and Shame System

In this *tautuaileva* reading, Matt 7:24–8:22 shows Jesus challenging the honor and shame system held by people of high status in the Jewish religious system, the Roman imperial system, and the local family system. This challenge shows a movement in-between spaces and the language in that transition is the rhetoric of praise (honor) and blame (shame). The narrator's depiction of Jesus's request for the type of listener he desires is presented in the language of praise and blame. This request exhibits one of the social ways of communication in the first century Mediterranean world which is "challenge and riposte." Challenge and riposte as social communication, is how first century Mediterranean people dialogued or argued on certain public subjects and issues. Those who did well in these debates were respected and honored.

Jesus's words in 7:24–29 is accordingly a challenge put forward to the crowd to help them come out of the oppressive situations in which they are trapped. Listening to Jesus's proclamation of ἡ βασιλεία τῶν οὐρανῶν and acting upon it, is developed in the parable of the wise and fool in 7:24–27. Jesus'schallenge is presented in forensic and deliberative speeches with an epideictic sense, according to which listening with actions is for the people in the present, in the past, and in the future. This presumes the presence of God in the lives of people in the past, present, and future.

The forensic speech in the aorist indicative tenses (ᾠκοδόμησεν, built; κατέβη, fell; ἦλθον, came; ἔπνευσαν, blew; προσέπεσαν, beat against; ἔπεσεν, fell), presents house building, and its after-effect, as an activity that was completed in the past. Forensic speech is defensive language, and that defensive mood is shown in the image of the impact of the winds, rain, and river on the houses built by the wise and the fool. The type of houses built, determines the type of defense against wind and rain.

The parable of the wise and the fool exhibits the difference between a wise and foolish decision. The word ὁμοιωθήσε (will be likened) is in the future indicative passive tense (7:24). It suggests that the type of listener Jesus speaks about is not just a person of the past and the present. S/he is also a person of the future. More importantly, the distinction between the wise and fool reveals the epideictic sense of the unit. The phrase "Everyone who hears these words of mine and acts on them will be like a wise man who built his house on the rock" (7:24) is an expression of praise. The one who hears and acts, is praised as wise. The wise is a person of honor and his reward is that his house stands strongly against the wind and rain. On the other hand, blame is heard in "And everyone who hears these words of mine and does not act on them will be like a foolish man who built his house on the sand" (7:26). The fool is a person of shame, whose house fell when the floods came, and the winds blew. Thus, the wise (as honorable) listens and acts upon Jesus's vision of the βασιλεία of the heaven while the fool (as shameful) does not listen and is shown in Jesus's dealings with various members of the crowd in the rest of the unit.

The language of praise and blame is in the healing of the leper. As an unclean person, the leper possesses a shameful status in the Jewish religious household. This is encapsulated by his words, "Lord, if you choose, you can make me clean" (8:2). Jesus's positive response to the leper's approach for help and sending the leper to return and show himself to the priest exhibit the language of praise: "I do choose. Be made clean! See that you say nothing to anyone; but go and show yourself to the priest" (8:3–4). The leper is one example of a wise person for he rose to the challenge. He came out of the space where he was oppressed because of his condition. He entered a new space, an unfamiliar space, to seek help for his need so that his role as a member of the Jewish religious household could be reinstated. The leper's wise decision makes him a person with honor. Jesus's challenge to the crowd is inclusive: anyone in the crowd regardless of gender and status receives honor if s/he responds positively to his challenge.

The centurion, as explained above, is a person of honor in the eyes of the local people of Galilee not only because he has power and authority but also because he has wealth. The exchange between Jesus and the centurion is an example of a member of the crowd from a different local household who accepts and acts on Jesus's challenge. The centurion's decision to seek help from Jesus is a challenging decision in several ways. First, as a Roman leader who asks a Jew for help, he is a humiliation to the Romans. Second, as a master who leaves his house to seek help for his servant is disreputable. However, as suggested above, the role of the centurion as a father to his servant was important to him. As such, he comes across as a wise person. His wise decision is shown in his words, "Lord, my servant is lying at home paralyzed, in terrible distress" (8:5); "Lord, I am not worthy to have you come under my roof; but only speak the word, and my servant will be healed" (8:8). Jesus's response praises the wise decision by the centurion: "Truly I tell you, no one in Israel have I found such faith" (8:10); "Go; let it be done for you according to your faith" (8:13). Jesus praises the faith of the centurion and the greatness of that faith is compared to the people of Israel at the time. The centurion is rewarded with honor to do as he has asked. The centurion's servants received honor in ἡ βασιλεία τῶν οὐρανῶν.

The centurion is one example of a member of the crowd who left his space of comfort—in which he is free to get anything he wants—and enters an unfamiliar space to find help for his servants. He is an example of a local person who enters in-between spaces to fulfill his role as leader of his household. In their exchange, Jesus acted as the broker between God—as patron—and the centurion, his servants, and his household—as clients. Jesus's ministry reversed aspects of the social and cultural system of the first century which asserted the power and authority of Romans. Jesus showed that the honor ascribed to and acquired by the centurion is supported by military force which colonised and oppressed people, and which is shameful in ἡ βασιλεία τῶν οὐρανῶν. The centurion's positive response and humble approach made him one of the honorable persons in ἡ βασιλεία τῶν οὐρανῶν. In this way, the centurion as leader acts as servant by entering in-between spaces, an unfamiliar third space for him.

This culture of honor and shame is also reflected in the healing of Peter's mother-in-law. Jesus as the broker enters Peter's house. In the previous healing activities, members of the crowd moved out of their familiar space to enter the space where Jesus is located. In the case of Peter's mother-in-law, Jesus as a Galilean enters another person's house, with which he was not familiar. In his role as broker of the patron-client relationship between God and people, Jesus has no choice but to enter the house in which this woman is lying sick. In his own initiative, Jesus enters the space that restrains a client of the patron God, in order to help her. Jesus's touching this woman implies Jesus's praise of her. She silently acted in response to Jesus. She rose up and began to serve Jesus. This woman was a good *tautua*.

Coming to the Matthean recitation of Isa 53:4a in 8:17, the narrator shows a different language of praise and blame. Accepting Jesus's proclamation of ἡ βασιλεία τῶν οὐρανῶν does not automatically free one from all difficulties and problems in a local place. Instead, it is the beginning of moving away from oppressive life circumstances that have colonized one's life in a local place. This type of work requires helping others who are in the same situation. This task is a restless one. It requires courage, commitment, and endurance. As such, sacrifice and courage are the languages of praise in facing the challenge of listening and doing Jesus's proclamation of ἡ βασιλεία τῶν οὐρανῶν.

The language of praise and blame based on that sacrifice of the follower's time to attend to the needs of local people is pictured in Jesus's response to the scribe in Matt 8:19–20 and to one of his disciple in Matt 8:21–22. For the scribe, Jesus's response is not to criticise the scribe's request but to let the scribe know of the challenges of attending to the needs of those who need help. Jesus's mission involves no rest, unlike the foxes that have holes in which to rest. It is also the challenge put forward by Jesus to one of his disciples. For Jesus, the disciple will waste his time by going to his family as he is needed during the night. In these responses, language of honor and shame permeates.

Summary

The different households to which the sick belong (8:1–17) reflect the household systems that marginalized them. Jesus's calling the crowd to listen and act upon his proclamation of ἡ βασιλεία τῶν οὐρανῶν shows that Jesus's healing ministry was not just to the sick person but to the social, cultural, and religious forces that have oppressed the sick. Using the imagery of building a house as metaphor exhibits building and rebuilding of social, cultural, political, and religious systems that have placed the sick in shameful situations. The social and cultural analysis offered here reveals that Jesus's healing activities in 7:24–8:22 gives honor to local people of Galilee who were considered shameful in their households.

Conclusion

The *tautuaileva* reading of Matt 7:24–8:22 connects Jesus's ministry to Galilee to the analysis of Matt 4:12–25. The imagery of building a house is a metaphor to express the locality of Jesus's ministry in this part of the story. The innertextual analysis shows in and through the language, narration, and progression of the text that Jesus's ministry is mission to characters in certain households. The mission is performed by both words and actions. The Matthean recitation of Isa 53:4 affirms Jesus's ministry to the people of Galilee, showing that discipleship as a place-based ministry is not an easy task. It requires endurance and courage. The social and cultural textual analysis reveals how Jesus's healing activities reverse the honor and shame system of the first century Mediterranean world. Those who seek help in Jesus are sent back to their households as disciples sent back to build and rebuild their households in light of the proclamation of ἡ βασιλεία τῶν οὐρανῶν.

The *tautuaileva* reading of Matt 7:24–8:22 show characteristics of discipleship that are pertinent to the needs and rights of local people, and anyone who responds positively to Jesus's ministry becomes his disciple. Following Jesus does not mean a disciple has to abandon his/her household, for s/he needs to take help back to build and rebuild his/her household. In this way, going and making disciples in one's own family and community is another characteristic of becoming a disciple. It is one way to demonstrate one's sense of belonging (*faasinomaga*) to his/her family. It is not an easy task. Facing hardship as a member of a family is part of being a *tautua* to one's family. This includes having courage to move in-between spaces, choosing what will best help the needs of the family. Such a family member is a *tautuatoa*.

6.

CONCLUSION

As the processes of globalization compress time and space, people increasingly participate in multiple realities at the same time. The world is ever more fluid. This is apparent among Samoans who have had to adapt to the realities of life that they face in different cultural, social, economic, political, and religious situations. This fluidity and its connection to Christian discipleship, is reflected in this study.

One of the aims of this study is to give attention to Jesus's teaching often read as the prioritizing of the church. This attention is needed because one of the criticisms of the church in today's Samoan society is that its continued assertion of traditional discipleship, in which church is considered more important than family, instigates domestic problems such as poverty and broken relationships in local families. This study has also met a lack in the dominant studies of Jesus, which do not pay attention to Jesus's connection to family and household in local places. This study contributes to the significant studies undertaken by other scholars on Jesus and family in the gospels, and also to the development of Samoan theories and methods of biblical interpretation.

The two parts of the study reflect my attempt to meet these purposes. In part 1, I gave a brief review of the use of traditional methods of interpretation over Matthew's sense of discipleship. I explained that traditional methods depict discipleship with one dimensional emphasis on the global and ecclesiological realm. The traditional methods and their interpretations served the manifestation and maintenance of discipleship as such, but it has a weakness. Its global emphasis overlooks the needs of people in local communities and families. Thus, there is a need in biblical interpretation to establish ways to explore how discipleship might be understood through the framework of local places. This is made possible by the shift from traditional and classical methods of interpretations to methods that signify the world of readers. In this way, I converted the traditional-global perspective on discipleship into my Samoan perspective of considering the needs and rights of local people at the local level. My goal was not to nullify the traditional interpretations of discipleship but to explore other dimensions such as the consideration of the worlds of readers, including my Samoan world in Oceania.

Bringing my world and the world of the text together is no easy task. I drew on Gadamer's philosophical approach to emphasize the importance of "play" between the text and the reader, who approaches the text with his/her own presuppositions. I also employed Gadamer's concept of "fusion of two horizons" to clarify this "play." But this is not always a smooth process. Fusion is actually the result of the play between the reader and the text. In this, I drew on the post-colonial concept of hybridity. Hybridity enabled me to analyse the fluctuation in-between the margin and the centre as an opportunity for the marginalized to seek ways to fulfill their needs. I used this hybrid experience as a hermeneutic to analyse the marginalized in the text.

Postcolonialism is useful in defining my location as a reader in third space. I named that third space *tautuaileva.* This is my place in the Samoan society in and through my experience of being a *tautua* member of my family. My experience and understanding as *tautua* enabled me to identify the problem caused by the impact of traditional understanding of discipleship in the Samoan society. The traditional understanding of discipleship contradicts the values embedded in the culture of service in Samoan culture and in Jesus's ministry. From my *tautua* third space I identified two categories that became hermeneutical lenses to inform the selection and analyses of texts from Matthew. Those categories are *fa'asinomaga* (sense of belonging) and *tautuatoa* (courageous servant).

Fa'asinomaga reveals how the characters in the text are linked to the place encoded in the text. *Tautuatoa* shows the movement of different characters in the text as breaking away from familiar spaces in order to enter new spaces where help or opportunity exists. Thus, the lenses of *fa'asinomaga* and *tautua-toa* enabled me to see discipleship as a mission that gives primary attention to the needs and rights of local people, in particular those in desperate situations.

These lenses guided my selection and reading of Matt 4:12–25 and Matt 7:24–8:22. These texts have been and still are considered to contain traditional passages that express traditional discipleship in Matthew. Using sociorhetorical interpretation as a tool, I explored the language, narration, and progression of the chosen texts with special attention to three stages of textuality— innertextures, intertextures, and social and cultural textures.

In part 2 I offered *Tautuaileva* readings of the selected texts. In exploring the innertexture of Matt 4:12–25 through the lens of *fa'asinomaga* I found that the language, narration, and progression of the text establish Jesus's and the crowd's sense of belonging to Galilee. Jesus's dwelling in Galilee is significant in the consideration of Galilee as a local place where the local people and their needs are important to Jesus's ministry. Through the lens of *tautuatoa*, I interpreted the development of the crowd from the beginning to the end of the unit as showing examples of local people (such as the fishermen) who break away from their familiar spaces to enter new spaces in search of ways to improve their situations.

The analysis of Matthew's recitation of Isa 8:23–9:1 shows affirmation of Jesus's belonging to Galilee. It is not just the place where Jesus's ministry began but also where Jesus dealt with the needs of the local people. The Isaian intertexture places Jesus's ministry within God's plan. This was clarified further in the analysis of the social and cultural textures of Matt 4:12–25 according to which Jesus's proclamation of ἡ βασιλεία τῶν οὐρανῶν reverses the honor and shame system which controlled and ruled the lives of the local people. With the lenses of *fa'asinomaga* and *tautuatoa*, the importance of Galilee as a local place in Jesus's ministry emerges strongly. Jesus's proclamation of discipleship began in a local place according to certain needs of the people in that place. This was made clearer in the analysis of Matt 7:24–8:22.

Through the lens of *fa'asinomaga* I demonstrated that Matt 7:24–8:22 shows Jesus and the characters in this text to have a sense of belonging to the local place of Galilee by means of the households to which they belonged. Jesus shows the importance of households in the parable of the wise and foolish builders. Through the lens of *tautuatoa* I saw the type of listener Jesus preferred to be a courageous servant—one who is prepared to move into unfamiliar places in search of opportunities to fulfill his/her role as servant. This type of listener emerged in the development of the movement of Jesus and his dealing with different characters. The healed are courageous servants. Jesus told some of the healed to return to their households, to help rebuild their households in accordance with the ἡ βασιλεία τῶν οὐρανῶν he has proclaimed.

Jesus as healer and the healed as *tautuatoa* are affirmed in Matthew's recitation of Isa 8:23–9:1. As shown in the *tautuaileva* reading above, the servant of God is someone whose mission is to help others take away their own suffering. This task is not easy and it requires a lot of the servant's time and energy. The social and cultural textual analysis amplifies this interpretation by demonstrating how Jesus's proclamation of ἡ βασιλεία τῶν οὐρανῶν honors the healed with a place in the household of God. Echoing the analysis of Matt 4:12–25, I showed in the analysis of Matt 7:24–8:22 that the Matthean story reveals the importance of attending to the needs and rights of local people. Discipleship begins from below or from the local level. In other words, the consideration of the needs and rights of local people determines the growth of the word of God at the global level.

Overall, the study has three features which are useful in developing methods of biblical interpretation in Samoa, in the study of discipleship in Matthew, and in the consideration of the teaching and practice of discipleship.

First, my approach, alongside Leota's, Mariota's, and Smith's, signifies the social, cultural, political, religious, and economic situations that Samoan people encounter in their everyday lives. As shown in this study, exposing the marginalized in my world and the world of the text is determined by a methodology that is informed by my identifying the problem that cause marginalization. I can employ the *tautuaileva* approach to read other texts in the Matthean account: First, Matt 9:2–8 speaks of Jesus's healing of the paralytic whom Jesus sends back to his family. Second, Matt 10:1–42 in which Jesus sends the twelve to the people of Israel, in a mission especially aimed at the households of the Jews. Third, the commissioning of the disciples in Matt 28:16–20 to go and make disciples of all nations.

Second, one of the aims of this study was to revisit discipleship and interpret it anew, privileging the needs and rights of local people. Traditional understanding of discipleship that focuses on building the church at the global level should not overlook the needs and rights of local people. Very important in this reading is the place of Galilee encoded in the text.

Third, further attention needs to be given to the role of the church in considering the needs and rights of local people. According to the interpretation presented here, discipleship is based on the situations of the local people. This type of ministry has been announced in and through the prophets. For the followers of Christ in Samoan societies, commitments to the church are important but so are the commitments to families. Ultimately, it is the family member's decision on what needs and commitments are to be given priority. This is not an easy task. It requires listening, speaking, and action. As I have suggested, Jesus gave the (healed) person in need the opportunity to reinstate himself or herself into the community but s/he has to make that opportunity available. For a family member to become a *tautua* requires courage to enter unfamiliar spaces. In this study, that is what it means to participate in *tautuaileva* (service in-between spaces).

This study has shown that Jesus's dealing with the needs and rights of local people can translate into the reality that we now encounter. It also demonstrates how local people as *tautua* of God and of their families may deal with their own needs and rights as members of their families, churches, and communities. In this way, discipleship is to be carried out in accordance with the needs and rights of people at the local level, upon which the (re)building of the church at the global level may begin.

BIBLIOGRAPHY

Anae, Melanie S. "Fofoaivaoese: Identity Journeys of NZ-born Samoans." PhD Dissertation, University of Auckland, 1998.

Anderson, Janice C. "Matthew: Gender and Reading." *Semeia* 28 (1983): 3–27.

Anderson, S. D. "Egalitarianism." *EBCE*, 128–129.

Ashcroft, Bill, Gareth Griffiths, and Helen Tiffin. *Post-Colonial Studies: The Key Concepts*. London: Routledge, 2000.

Aristotle. *Art of Rhetoric*. Translated by J. H. Freese. Massachusetts: Harvard, 1991.

Bailey, James L., and Lyle D. Vander Broek. *Literary Forms in the New Testament: A Handbook*. Louisville: Westminster John Knox, 1992.

Barton, Stephen C. *Discipleship and Family Ties in Mark and Matthew*. SNTSMS 80. Cambridge: Cambridge University Press, 1994.

Bauckham, Richard. "Egalitarianism and Hierarchy in the Biblical Traditions." Pages 259–273 in *Interpreting the Bible: Historical and Theological Studies in Honour of David F. Wright*. Edited by Anthony N. S. Lane. Leicester: Inter-Varsity, 1997.

———. "The Son of Man: a 'Man in My Position' or 'Someone'?" *JSNT* 23 (1985): 23–33.

Bauer, David R. *The Structure of Matthew's Gospel: A Study in Literary Design*. Sheffield: Sheffield Academic, 1988.

Beavis, Mary A. "Christians Origins, Egalitarianism and Utopia." *JFSR* 23 (2007): 27–49.

Bermejo-Rubio, Fernando. "(Why) Was Jesus the Galilean Crucified Alone? Solving a False Conundrum." *JSNT* 36.2 (2013): 127–54.

Bhabha, Homi. *The Location of Culture*. London: Routledge, 1994.

Black, Stephanie. *Sentence Conjunctions in the Gospel of Matthew: καί, δέ, τότε, γάρ, οὖν, and Asyndeton in Narrative Discourse*. Sheffield: Sheffield Academic, 2002.

Bosch, David J. *Transforming Mission: Paradigm Shifts in Theology of Mission*. Maryknoll: Orbis, 1996.

———. *Witness to the World: The Christian Mission in Theological Perspective*. London: Marshall Morgan & Scott, 1980.

Boring, M. Eugene. "The Convergence of Source Analysis, Social History, and Literary Structure in the Gospel of Matthew." Pages 587–611 in *Seminar Papers: Society of Biblical Literature Annual Meeting*. Georgia: Scholars Press, 1994.

Brown, Henry P. *Egalitarianism and the Generation of Inequality.* Oxford: Clarendon, 1988.

Brueggemann, Walter. *Isaiah 40–66.* NICOT. Louisville: Westminster John Knox, 1998.

———. *Theology of the Old Testament: Testimony, Dispute, Advocacy.* Minneapolis: Fortress, 1997.

Carter, Warren. "Evoking Isaiah: Matthean Soteriology and An Intertextual Reading of Isaiah 7–9 and Matthew 1:23 and 4:15–16." *JBL* 119 (2000): 503–20.

———. "Kernels and Narrative Blocks: The Structure of Matthew's Gospel." *CBQ* 54.3 (1992): 463–481.

———. *Matthew and Empire: Initial Explorations.* Harrisburg: Trinity Press International, 2001.

———. *Matthew and the Margins: A Socio-political and Religious Reading.* JSNTSup 204. Maryknoll: Orbis, 2000.

———. "Matthew 4:18–22 and the Matthean Discipleship: An Audience-Oriented Perspective." *CBQ* 59 (1997): 58–75.

———. *Matthew: Storyteller, Interpreter, Evangelist.* Peabody: Hendrickson, 1996.

Childs, Brevard S. *Isaiah.* OTL. Louisville: Westminster John Knox, 2001.

Choi, Naomi. "Egalitarianism." In *EPT*, 411–14.

Cousland, J. R. C. *The Crowds in the Gospel of Matthew.* NovTSup 102. Leiden: Brill, 2002.

Crosby, Michael H. *House of Disciples: Church, Economics, and Justice in Matthew.* Maryknoll: Orbis, 1988.

Davies, W. D., and Dale C. Allison. *A Critical and Exegetical Commentary on the Gospel according to Saint Matthew I–VII.* ICC. Edinburgh: T&T Clark, 1988.

———. *A Critical and Exegetical Commentary on the Gospel according to Saint Matthew VIII–XVIII.* ICC. Edinburgh: T&T Clark, 1991.

deSilva, David A. *Honor, Patronage, Kinship and Purity: Unlocking New Testament Culture.* Downers Grove: InterVarsity, 2000.

Dube, Musa W. "Go Therefore and Make Disciples of All Nations" (Matt 8:19a): A Postcolonial Perspective on Biblical Criticism and Pedagogy." Pages 224–246 in *Teaching the Bible: The Discourses and Politics of Biblical Pedagogy.* Edited by. Fernando F. Segovia and Mary Ann Tobert. Maryknoll: Orbis, 1998.

———. *Postcolonial Feminist Interpretation of the Bible.* St. Louis: Chalice Press, 2000.

———. "Who Do You Say that I am?" FTh 15.3 (2007): 346–67.

Duling, Dennis C. *A Marginal Scribe: Studies in the Gospel of Matthew in a Social-Scientific Perspective.* Eugene: Cascade, 2011.

————. "The Matthean Brotherhood and Marginal Scribal Leadership." Pages 159–82 in *Modelling Early Christianity: Social-Scientific Studies of the New Testament in Its Context.* Edited by Philip F. Esler. London: Routledge, 1995.

————. "The Therapeutic Son of David: An Element in Matthew's Christological Apologetic." *NTS* 24.3 (1978): 392–410.

Edwards, Richard A. *Matthew's Narrative Portrait of Disciples: How the Text-Connoted Reader Is Informed.* Harrisburg: Trinity Press International, 1997.

————. "Uncertain Faith: Matthew's Portrait of the Disciples." Pages 47–61 in *Discipleship in the New Testament.* Edited by Fernando F. Segovia. Philadelphia: Fortress, 1985.

Efi, Tui Atua Tupua Tamasese Ta'isi. "Keynote Address for Pacific Futures Law and Religion Symposium." National University of Samoa, Lepapaigalagala, Samoa 3 December 2008, accessed at http://www.head-of-state-samoa.ws/pages/welcome.html 14 July 2013.

Elliott, John H. *A Home for the Homeless: A Sociological Exegesis of 1 Peter, Its Situation and Strategy.* London: SCM, 1990.

————. "Jesus Was Not an Egalitarian: A Critique of an Anachronistic and Idealist Theory." *BTB* 32 (2002): 75–91.

————. "The Jesus Movement Was Not Egalitarian but Family-Oriented." *BibInt* 11.2 (2003): 173–210.

————. *What Is Social-Scientific Criticism?* Minneapolis: Fortress, 1993.

Engler, Steven. "Tradition's Legacy." Pages 357–78 in *Historicizing Tradition in the Study of Religion.* Edited by Steven Engler and Gregory P. Grieve. New York: de Gruyter, 2005.

Ernst, Manfred. *Winds of Change: Rapidly Growing Religious Groups in the Pacific Islands.* Suva: Pacific Conference of Churches, 1994.

Ete, Risatisone. "Ugly Duckling, Quacking Swan." Pages 43–48 in *Faith in a Hyphen: Cross-Cultural Theologies Down Under.* Edited by Clive Pearson and Jione Havea. Adelaide: Openbook Publishers, 2005.

Evans, Craig A. *Matthew.* NCBC. Cambridge: Cambridge University Press, 2012.

Farnell, David F. "The Synoptic Gospels in the Ancient Church: The Testimony to the Priority of Matthew's Gospel." *MSJ* 10 (1999): 53–86.

Fau'olo, Oka. *O Vavega o le Alofa Lavea'i: O le tala faasolopito o le Ekalesia Faapotopotoga Kerisiano i Samoa.* Apia: Malua Printing Press, 2005.

Fishelov, David. "Types of Characters, Characteristics of Types." *Style* 24.3 (1990): 422–39.

Foster, Robert. "Why on Earth Use 'Kingdom of Heaven'?: Matthew's Terminology Revisited." *NTS* 48.4 (2002): 487–99.

France, R. T. *The Gospel of Matthew.* NICNT. Grand Rapids: Eerdmans, 2007.

Freyne, Sean. *Galilee, Jesus and the Gospels: Literary Approaches and Historical Investigations.* Philadelphia: Fortress, 1988.

———. *Galilee and Gospel: Collected Essays.* WUNT 125. Tübingen: Mohr, 2000.

———. "Herodian Economics in Galilee: Searching for a Suitable Model." Pages 23–46 in *Modelling Early Christianity: Social-Scientific Studies of the New Testament in Its Context.* Edited by Philip F. Esler. New York: Routledge, 1995.

———. *Jesus, A Jewish Galilean: A New Reading of the Jesus-Story.* London: T&T Clark International, 2004.

Gadamer, Hans-Georg. *Truth and Method.* Translated by Joel Weinsheimer and Donald G. Marshall. New York: Seabury Press, 1975.

Gilroy, Paul. *Between Camps: Nations, Cultures and the Allure of Race.* London: Routledge, 2004.

Gilson, R. P. *Samoa 1830–1900: The Politics of a Multi-Cultural Community.* Melbourne: Oxford University Press, 1970.

Good, Deidre. "The Verb ΑΝΑΧΩΡΕΩ in Matthew's Gospel." *NovT* 32 (1990):1–12.

Government of Samoa, *The Constitution of the Independent State of Western Samoa.* Apia: Samoa Printing and Publishing Co. Ltd., 1960.

Grant, Ken A. "Living in the Borderlands: An Identity and a Proposal." *Di* 49 1 (2010): 26–33.

Gundry, Robert H. *Matthew: A Commentary on His Handbook for a Mixed Church under Persecution.* 2nd ed. Grand Rapids: Eerdmans, 1994.

———. *Matthew: A Commentary on His Literary and Theological Art.* Grand Rapids: Eerdmans, 1982.

———. "A Responsive Evaluation of the Social History of the Matthean Community in Roman Syria." Pages 189–200 in *Social History of the Matthean Community: Cross-Disciplinary Approaches.* Edited by David L. Balch. Minneapolis: Fortress, 1991.

———. "On True and False Disciples in Matthew 8.18–22." *NTS* 40.3 (1994): 433–41.

Hagner, Donald A. *Matthew 1–13.* WBC 33a. Nashville: Thomas Nelson, 2000.

Hannan, Margaret. *The Nature and Demands of the Sovereign Rule of God in the Gospel of Matthew.* New York: T&T Clark International, 2006.

Hanson, K. C. "The Galilean Fishing Economy and the Jesus Tradition." *BTB* 27.3 (1997): 99–111.

Hanson, K. C., and Douglas E. Oakman. *Palestine in the Time of Jesus.* Minneapolis: Fortress, 1998.

Hare, Douglas R. A. "How Jewish Is the Gospel of Matthew?" *CBQ* 62.2 (2000): 264–77.

Harrington, Daniel J. *The Gospel of Matthew*. Sacra Pagina. Collegeville: Liturgical Press, 2007.

Havea, Jione. "The Future Stands between Here and There: Towards and Island(ic) Hermeneutics," *PJT* 2.13 (1995): 61–68.

———. "Numbers." Pages 43–51 in *Global Bible Commentary*. Edited by Daniel Patte. Nashville: Abingdon, 2004.

———, ed. *Sea of Readings: The Bible in the South Pacific*. Atlanta: SBL Press, forthcoming.

———. "Shifting the Boundaries: House of God and Politics of reading." *PJT* 2.16 (1996): 55–57.

Havea, Jione, Margaret Aymer, and Steed Vernyl Davidson, eds. *Islands, Islanders, and the Bible: RumInations*. Atlanta: SBL Press, 2015.

Hengel, Martin. *The Charismatic Leader and His Followers*. Translated by James C. G. Greig. Edinburg: T&T Clark, 1981.

———. "The Effective History of Isaiah 53 in the Pre-Christian Period." Pages 75–146 in *The Suffering Servant: Isaiah 53 in Jewish and Christian Sources*. Edited by Bernd Janowski and Peter Stuhlmacher. Grand Rapids: Eerdmans, 2004.

Hill, David. "Son and Servant: An Essay on Mathean Christology." *JSNT* 6 (1980): 2–16.

———. *The Gospel of Matthew*. NCB. London: Butler & Tanner, 1972.

Holtug Nils., and Lippert-Ramussen Kasper, eds. *Egalitarianism: New Essays on the Nature and Value of Equality*. Oxford: Clarendon, 2007.

Horsley, Richard A. *Archaeology, History and Society in Galilee: The Social Context of Jesus and the Rabbis*. Harrisburg: Trinity Press International, 1996.

———. *Galilee: History, Politics, People*. Valley Forge: Trinity Press International, 1995.

———. *Sociology and the Jesus Movement*. New York: Crossroad, 1989.

———. "Synagogues in Galilee and the Gospels." Pages 46–69 in *Evolution of the Synagogue: Problems and Progress*. Edited by Howard Clark Kee and Lynn H. Cohick. Harrisburg: Trinity Press International, 1999.

Horsley, Richard A., and John S. Hanson. *Bandits, Prophets, and Messiahs: Popular Movements in the Time of Jesus*. Minneapolis: Winston, 1985.

Howell, David B. *Matthew's Inclusive Story: A Study in the Narrative Rhetoric of the First Gospel*. JSNTSup 42. Sheffield: Sheffield Academic, 1990.

Hultgren, Arland J. *The Parables of Jesus: A Commentary*. Grand Rapids: Eerdmans, 2000.

Hutnyk, John. "Hybridity." *ERS* 28 (2005): 79–102.

Jacobs-Malina, Diane. *Beyond Patriarchy: The Images of Family in Jesus*. New York: Paulist Press, 1993.

Jennings, W., and Tat-Siong Benny Liew. "Mistaken Identities but Model Faith: Rereading the Centurion, the Chap, and the Christ in Matthew 8:5–13." *JBL* 123 (2004): 467–94.

Jensen, Morten H. "Rural Galilee and Rapid Changes: An Investigation of the Socio-economic Dynamics and Developments in Roman Galilee." *Biblica* 93 (2012): 43–67.

Jeremias, Joachim. *The Parables of Jesus.* NTL. London: SCM Press, 1963.

Joubert, Stephan F. "Managing the Household: Paul as *Paterfamilias* of the Christian Household Group in Corinth." Pages 213–23 in *Modelling Early Christianity: Social-Scientific Studies of the New Testament in Its Context.* Edited by Philip F. Esler. New York: Routledge, 1995.

Kamu, Lalomilo. *The Samoan Culture and The Christian Gospel.* Suva: Methodist Printing Press, 1996.

Keener, Craig S. *The Gospel of Matthew: A Socio-rhetorical Commentary.* Grand Rapids: Eerdmans, 2009.

Kennedy, George. *New Testament Interpretation through Rhetorical Criticism.* Chapel Hill: University of North Carolina Press, 1984.

———. *Progymnasmata: Greek Textbooks of Prose Composition and Rhetoric.* Atlanta: SBL, 2003.

Kent, Susan. "Egalitarianism, Equality, and Equitable Power." Pages 30–48 in *Manifesting Power: Gender and Interpretation of Power in Archaeology.* Edited by Tracy L. Sweely. London: Routledge, 1999.

Kingsbury, Jack D. *Matthew as Story.* 2nd ed. Philadelphia: Fortress, 1988.

———. *Matthew: Structure, Christology, Kingdom.* Philadelphia: Fortress, 1975.

———. "The Figure of Jesus in Matthew's Story: A Literary-Critical Probe." *JSNT* 21 (1984): 3–36.

———. "The Figure of Jesus in Matthew's Story A Rejoinder to David Hill." *JSNT* 25 (1985): 61–81.

———. "On Following Jesus: The 'Eager' Scribe and the 'Reluctant' Disciple (Matthew 8:18–22)." *NTS* 34 (1988): 45–59.

———. "The Miracle of the Cleansing of the Leper as an approach to the theology of Matthew." *CurTM* 4.6 (1977): 344–49.

———. *The Parables of Jesus in Matthew 13: A Study in Redaction Criticism.* London: SPCK, 1978.

———. "The Verb *AKOLOUTHEIN* ("To Follow") as an Index of Matthew's View of his Community." *JBL* 97 (1978): 56–73.

Kitiona, Lealaiauloto Nofoaiga and Tauiliili, Fuataga L. *O le Faavae o Samoa Anamua.* Apia: Malua Printing Press, 1985.

Kupp, David D. *Matthew's Emmanuel: Divine Presence and God's People in the First Gospel.* SNTSMS 90. Cambridge: Cambridge University Press, 1996.

Le Tagaloa, Aiono F. *O le Fa'asinomaga: Le Tagata ma lona Fa'asinomaga.* Alafua: Lamepa, 1997.

Leota, Peni. "Ethnic Tensions in Persian-Period Yehud: A Samoan Postcolonial Hermeneutic." PhD Thesis, Melbourne College of Divinity, 2005.

Letter Two. "Charity and the Church." In *Samoa Observer Newspaper*, 5 February 2012.

Letter Three. "Criticism against the Church." In *Samoa Observer Newspaper*, 25 February 2012.

Letter One. "Such a Meaningless Statement from Rev Vaiao Eteuati." In *Samoa Observer Newspaper*, 29 January 2012.

Levine, Amy-Jill. *The Social and Ethnic Dimensions of Matthean Social History: "Go nowhere among the Gentiles..." (Matt. 10:5b).* Lewiston: Edwin Mellon, 1988.

Lohr, Charles H. "Oral Techniques in the Gospel of Matthew." *CBQ* 23.4 (1961): 403–35.

Luzbetak, Louis J. *The Church and Cultures: New Perspectives in Missiological Anthropology.* Maryknoll: Orbis, 1989.

Luz, Ulrich. *Matthew 1–7.* Translated by James E. Crouch. Minneapolis: Fortress, 2007.

———. *Matthew 8–20.* Translated by James E. Crouch. Minneapolis: Fortress, 2001.

———. *Studies in Matthew.* Translated by Rosemary Selle. Grand Rapids: Eerdmans 2005.

———. "The Son of Man in Matthew: Heavenly Judge or Human Christ." *JSNT* 48 (1992): 3–21.

MacIntyre, Alasdair. "The Virtues, the Unity of a Human Life and the Concept of a Tradition." Pages 89–110 in *Why Narrative?* Edited by Stanley Hauerwas and L. Gregory Jones. Grand Rapids: Eerdmans, 1989.

Mack, Burton L. *Rhetoric and the New Testament.* Minneapolis: Fortress, 1990.

Macpherson, Cluny, and Laavasa Macpherson. *The Warm Winds of Change: Globalisation in Contemporary Samoa.* Auckland: Auckland University Press, 2009.

Mageo, Jeannette M. *Theorizing Self in Samoa: Emotions, Genders, and Sexualities.* Michigan: The University of Michigan Press, 1998.

Mailo, Mosese. *Bible-ing My Samoan: Native Language and the Politics of Bible Translating in the Nineteenth Century.* Apia: Piula Publications, 2016.

Malina, Bruce J. *The New Testament World: Insights from Cultural Anthropology.* Minneapolis: Fortress, 1993.

———. "Understanding New Testament Persons." Pages 41–61 in *The Social Sciences and New Testament Interpretation.* Edited by Richard Rohrbaugh. Peabody: Hendrickson, 1996.

Malina, Bruce J., and Jerome H. Neyrey. *Calling Jesus Names: The Social Value of Labels in Matthew.* Sonoma: Polebridge Press, 1988.

Mariota, Martin W. "A Samoan *Palagi* Reading of Exodus 2–3." MTh Thesis, University of Auckland, 2012.

Massey, Doreen. *Space, Place and Gender.* Cambridge: Polity, 1994.

Mayhew, Susan. *A Dictionary of Geography.* Oxford: Oxford University Press, 1997.

Meier, John. *Matthew.* Dublin: Veritas Publications, 1980.

Meleisea, Malama. *Change and Adaptations in Western Samoa.* Canterbury: University of Canterbury, 1992.

———. *Lagaga: A Short History of Western Samoa.* Suva: University of the South Pacific Press, 1987.

Menken, Maarten J. J. "The Source of the Quotation from Isaiah 53:4 in Matthew 8:17." *NovT* 39.4 (1997), 313–27.

Meyers, Eric M. "Ancient Synagogues: An Archaeological Introduction." Pages 3–20 in *Sacred Realm: The Emergence of the Synagogue in the Ancient World.* Edited by Steven Fine. Oxford: Oxford University Press, 1996.

Milner, G. B. *Samoan Dictionary: Samoan-English, English-Samoan.* Oxford: Oxford University Press, 1966.

Minear, Paul S. "The Disciples and the Crowds in the Gospel of Matthew." *AThR* 3 (1974): 28–44.

Moxnes, Halvor. "Honor and Shame." Pages 19–40 in *The Social Sciences and New Testament Interpretation.* Edited by Richard Rohrbaugh. Peabody: Hendrickson, 1996.

———. "Identity in Jesus' Galilee: From Ethnicity to Locative Intersectionality." *BibInt* 18.4–5 (2010): 390–416.

———. "Landscape and Spatiality: Placing Jesus." Pages 90–106 in *Understanding the Social World of the New Testament.* Edited by Dietmar Neufeld and Richard E. DeMaris. New York: Routledge, 2010.

———. *Putting Jesus in His Place: A Radical Vision of Household and Kingdom.* Louisville: Westminster John Knox, 2003.

———. "The Construction of Galilee as a Place for the Historical Jesus: Part I." *BTB* 31 (2001): 26–37.

———. "The Construction of Galilee as a Place for the Historical Jesus: Part II." *BTB* 31 (2001): 64–77.

Murphy-O'Connor, Jerome. "Fishers of Fish, Fishers of Men." *BRev* 15.3 (1999): 22–49.

Myers, Ched. *Binding the Strong Man: A political Reading of Mark's Story of Jesus.* Maryknoll: Orbis, 1988.

Neyrey, Jerome H. *Honor and Shame in the Gospel of Matthew.* Louisville: Westminster John Knox, 1998.

————. "Loss of Wealth, Loss of Family and Loss of Honor: The Cultural Context of the Original Makarisms in Q." Pages 139–158 in *Modelling Early Christianity: Social-Scientific Studies of the New Testament in Its Context.* Edited by Philip F. Esler. New York: Routledge, 1995.

Ngan-Woo, Feleti E. *Fa'aSamoa: The World of Samoans.* Auckland: Office of Race Relations Conciliator, 1985.

Nofoaiga, Vaitusi. "Jesus the *Fiaola* (Opportunity Seeker): Hybrid Samoan Reading of Matthew 8:1–17." In *Sea of Readings: The Bible and the South Pacific.* Edited by Jione Havea. SBL Press: Forthcoming.

Nolland, John. *The Gospel of Matthew: A Commentary on the Greek text.* NIGTC. Grand Rapids: Eerdmans, 2005.

Novakovic, Lidija "Matthew's Atomistic Use of the Scripture: Messianic Interpretation of Isaiah 53:4 in Matthew 8:17." Pages 147–62 in vol. 2 of *Biblical Interpretation in Early Christian Gospels.* Edited by Thomas R. Hatina. London: T&T Clark International, 2008.

Ortner, Sherry B. *Making Gender: The Politics and Erotics of Culture.* Boston: Beacon, 1996.

Oswalt, John N. *The Book of Isaiah Chapters 40–66.* NICOT. Grand Rapids: Eerdmans, 1998.

Overman, J. Andrew. *Church and Community in Crisis: The Gospel according to Matthew.* Pennsylvania: Trinity Press International, 1996.

————. *Matthew's Gospel and Formative Judaism: The Social World of the Matthean Community.* Minneapolis: Fortress, 1990.

Pamment, Margaret. "The Kingdom of Heaven according to the First Gospel." *NTS* 27.2 (1981): 211–32.

Panapa, Fereti S. "The Significance of Hospitality in the Traditions of the First Testament and Its Parallels to the Samoan Culture of Talimalo." MTh Thesis, University of Auckland, 2000.

Park, Sophia, S.N.J.M. "The Galilean Jesus: Creating a Borderland at the Foot of the Cross (Jn 19:23–30)." *TS* 70 (2009): 419–36.

Patte, Daniel. *Discipleship according to the Sermon on the Mount.* Valley Forge: Trinity Press International, 1996.

Perelini, Otele. "A Comparison of Jesus' Healing with Healing in Traditional and Christian Samoa." PhD Dissertation, Edinburg University, 1992.

Pilch, John J., and Bruce J. Malina., eds. *Handbook of Biblical Social Values.* Peabody: Hendrickson, 1980.

Powell, Mark. *What Is Narrative Criticism?* Minneapolis: Fortress, 1990.

Ranajit, Guha, ed. *A Subaltern Studies Reader, 1986–1995.* Minneapolis: University of Minnesota Press, 1997.

Richardson, Peter. *Herod: King of the Jews and Friend of the Romans.* Columbia: University of South Carolina Press, 1996.

Robbins, Vernon K. *Exploring the Texture of Texts: A Guide to Socio-rhetorical Interpretation.* Harrisburg: Trinity, 1996.
————. *The Invention of Christian Discourse.* Vol. 1. Blandform Forum: Deo, 2009.
————. *The Tapestry of Early Christian Discourse: Rhetoric, Society and Ideology.* New York: Routledge, 1996.
Roth, John K., ed. *International Encyclopaedia of Ethics.* Chicago: Salem Press, 1995.
Runesson, Anna. *Exegesis in the Making: Postcolonialism and New Testament Studies.* Leiden: Brill, 2011.
Saldarini, Anthony J. *Matthew's Christian-Jewish Community.* Chicago: University of Chicago Press, 1994.
————. "The Gospel of Matthew and Jewish-Christian Conflict." Pages 38–61 in *Social History of the Matthean Community: Cross-Disciplinary Approaches.* Edited by David L. Balch. Minneapolis: Fortress, 1991.
Sandnes, Karl Olav. "Equality Within Patriarchal Structures: Some New Testament Perspectives on the Christian Fellowship as a Brother- or Sisterhood and Family." Pages 150–65 in *Constructing Early Christian Families: Family as Social Reality and Metaphor.* Edited by Halvor Moxnes. London: Routledge, 1997.
Said, Edward. *Orientalism: Western Conceptions of the Orient.* London: Penguin Books, 1978.
Schoeffel, Penelope. "The Samoan Concept of *Feagaiga* and its Transformation." Pages 85–105 in *Tonga and Samoa: Images of Gender and Polity.* Edited by Judith Huntsman. Canterbury: University of Canterbury, 1995.
Schweizer, Eduard. *The Good News according to Matthew.* Translated by David E. Green. London: Westminster John Knox, 1975.
Schüssler Fiorenza, Elizabeth. *Discipleship of Equals: A Critical Feminist Ekklesia-ology of Liberation.* London: SCM, 1993.
————. "The Oratory of Euphemia and *Ekklesia* of Wo/man." Pages 3–32 in *Jesus: Miriam's Child, Sophia's Prophet.* New York: Continuum, 1995.
Segovia, Frenando F. "And They Began to Speak in Other Tongues: Competing Modes of Discourse in Contemporary Biblical Criticism." Pages 1–34 in vol. 1 of *Reading from This Place: Social Location and Biblical Interpretation in the United States.* Edited by Fernando Segovia and Mary Ann Tolbert. Minneapolis: Fortress, 1995.
————. "Cultural Studies and Contemporary Biblical Criticism: Ideological Criticism as Mode of Discourse." Pages 1–17 in vol. 2 of *Reading from This Place: Social Location and Biblical Interpretation in Global Perspective.* Edited by Fernando F. Segovia and Mary Ann Tolbert. Minneapolis: Fortress, 1995.

————. *Decolonizing Biblical Studies: A View from the Margins.* New York: Orbis, 2000.

————. "Introduction: Call and Discipleship: Toward a Re-examination of the Shape and Character of Christian Existence in the New Testament." Pages 1–23 in *Discipleship in the New Testament.* Edited by Fernando F. Segovia. Philadelphia: Fortress, 1985.

————. "Postcolonial Criticism and the Gospel of Matthew." Pages 194–237 in *Methods of Matthew.* Edited by Mark Allan Powell. Cambridge: Cambridge University Press, 2009.

————. "Toward Interculturalism: Reading Strategy from the Diaspora." Pages 321–30 in vol. 2 of *Reading from This Place: Social Location and Biblical Interpretation in Global Perspective.* Edited by Fernando F. Segovia and Mary Ann Tolbert. Minneapolis: Fortress, 1995.

Shore, Bradd. "Sexuality and Gender in Samoa: Conceptions and Missed Conceptions." Pages 192–215 in *Sexual Meaning: The Cultural Construction of Gender and Sexuality.* Edited by Sherry B. Ortner and Harriet Whitehead. Cambridge: Cambridge University Press, 1981.

Slingerland, H. Dixon. "The Transjordanian Origin of St. Matthew's Gospel." *JSNT* 18.3 (1979): 18–28.

Smith, Frank. "The Johannine Jesus from a Samoan Perspective: Towards an Intercultural Reading of the Fourth Gospel." PhD Thesis, University of Auckland, 2010.

Spivak, Gayatri C. "Can the Subaltern Speak?" Pages 271–314 in *Marxism and the Interpretation of Culture.* Edited by Cary Nelson and Lawrence Grossberg. Urbana: University of Illinois Press, 1988.

Stanton, Graham N. "Revisiting Matthew's Communities." *HvTSt* 52 (1996): 376–94.

Sugirtharajah, R. S. *Asian Biblical Hermeneutics and Postcolonialism: Contesting Interpretation.* Sheffield: Sheffield Academic, 1998.

————. "A Postcolonial Exploration of Collusion and Construction in Biblical Interpretation." Pages 91–116 in *The Postcolonial Bible.* Edited by R. S. Sugirtharajah. Sheffield: Sheffield Academic, 1998.

————. *Postcolonial Criticism and Biblical Interpretation.* Oxford: Oxford University Press, 2002.

————. "Vernacular Resurrections: An Introduction." Pages 11–17 in *Vernacular Hermeneutics.* Edited by R. S. Sugirtharajah. Sheffield: Sheffield Academic, 1999.

————, ed. *Vernacular Hermeneutics.* Sheffield: Sheffield Academic, 1999.

Talapusi, Faitala. "Jesus Christ in the Pacific World of Spirits." BD Thesis, Pacific Theological College, 1976.

Tapua'i, Fa'atauvaa. "A Comparative Study of the Samoan Study of the Samoan and Hebrew Concepts of the Covenant." BD Thesis, Pacific Theological College, 1972.

Taylor, Charles *Philosophy and the Human Sciences: Philosophical Papers.* Cambridge: Cambridge University Press, 1985.

Theissen, Gerd. "Itinerant Radicalism: The Tradition of Jesus' Sayings from the Perspective of the Sociology of Literature." *RR* 2 (1975): 84–93.

———. *The First Followers of Jesus: A Sociological Analysis of the Earliest Christianity.* Translated by John Bowden. London: SCM, 1978.

Thiselton, Anthony S. *The Two Horizons: New Testament Hermeneutical Philosophical Description with Special Reference to Heidegger, Bultmann, Gadamer and Wittgenstein.* Exeter: Partenoster, 1980.

Tiatia, Jemaima. *Caught between Cultures: Aotearoa/New Zealand-Born Pacific Island Perspective.* Ellerslie: Christian Research Association, 1998.

Thornton, Alec., Tony Binns, and Maria Talaitupu Kerslake. "Hard Times in Apia? Urban Landlessness and the Church in Samoa." *SJTG* 34.3 (2013): 357–72.

Tofaeono, Ama'amalele. *Eco-Theology: Aiga The Household of Life - A Perspective from Living Myths and Traditions.* Erlangen: Erlangen Verlag für Mission Und Okumene, 2000.

Tucker, Gene M. *The Book of Isaiah 1–39.* NIB. Nashville: Abingdon Press, 2001.

Ukpong, Justin. "Inculturation Hermeneutics: An African Approach to Biblical Interpretation." Pages 17–32 in *The Bible in a World Context.* Edited by Walter Dietrich and Ulrich Luz. Grand Rapids: Eerdmans, 2002.

Vaai, Saleimoa, *Samoa Faamatai and the Rule of Law.* Apia: National University of Samoa Press, 1999.

Vaka'uta, Nasili. *Reading Ezra 9–10 Tu'a-Wise: Rethinking Biblical Interpretation in Oceania.* Atlanta: Society of Biblical Literature, 2011.

Van Tilborg, Sjef. *The Jewish Leaders in Matthew.* Leiden: Brill, 1972.

Wainwright, Elaine M. "Feminist Criticism and the Gospel of Matthew." Pages 83–117 in *Methods for Matthew.* Edited by Mark Allan Powell. Cambridge: Cambridge University Press, 2009.

———. "Reading Matthew 3–4: Jesus; Sage, Seer, Sophia, Son of God." *JSNT* 77 (2000): 25–43.

———*Shall We Look for Another? A Feminist Rereading of the Matthean Jesus.* Maryknoll: Orbis, 1998.

———. "The Matthean Jesus and the Healing of Women." Pages 74–95 in *The Gospel of Matthew in Current Study.* Edited by David E. Aune. Grand Rapids: Eerdmans, 2001.

———. *Towards a Feminist Critical Reading of the Gospel according to Matthew.* BZNW 60. Berlin: de Gruyter, 1991.

————. *Women Healing/Healing Women: The Genderization of Healing in Early Christianity.* London: Equinox, 2006.

————. "'Your Faith Has Made You Well': Jesus, Women, and Healing in the Gospel of Matthew." Pages 224–245 in *Transformative Encounters: Jesus and Women Re-viewed.* Edited by Ingrid Rosa Kitzberger. Leiden: Brill, 2000.

Waldrom, Jeremy. *God, Locke, and Equality: Christian Foundations in Locke's Political Thought.* Cambridge: Cambridge University Press, 2002.

Watts, John D. W. *Isaiah 1–33.* WBC. Texas: Word Books, 1985.

————. *Isaiah 34–66.* WBC. Texas: Word Books, 1987.

Wendt, Albert. *Sons for The Return Home.* Auckland: Penguin, 1973.

Wenham, J. W. *The Elements of New Testament Greek.* Cambridge: Cambridge University Press, 1996.

White, L. Michael. "Crisis Management and Boundary Maintenance: The Social Location of the Matthean Community." Pages 211–47 in *Social History of the Matthean Community: Cross-Disciplinary Approaches.* Edited by David L. Balch. Minneapolis: Fortress, 1991.

Wilkins, Michael J. *The Concept of Disciple in Matthew's Gospel: As Reflected in the Use of the Term μαθητῆς.* Leiden: Brill, 1988.

Wilson, Walter T. "The Uninvited Healer: Houses, Healing and Prophets in Matthew 8:1–22." *JSNT* 36.1 (2013): 53–72.

Wulf, Arthur John. "Was Earth Created Good? Reappraising Earth in Genesis 1:1–2:4a from a Samoan Perspective." PhD Thesis, University of Auckland, 2016.

Young, Robert. *Postcolonialism: An Historical Introduction.* Oxford: Blackwell, 2001.

————. *Colonial Desire: Hybridity in Theory, Culture and Race.* London: Routledge, 1995.

INDEX

Ingram Content Group UK Ltd.
Milton Keynes UK
UKHW010012010723
424392UK00003B/27